praise for thrift store coats

"From the valleys of Ohio and Kentucky on to the shores of Lake Erie and the Mississippi River, *Thrift Store Coats* explores the lives of characters who inhabit the Rust Belt and middle America. Each of these stories examines the ways in which our hometowns – and our homelands, as it were –indelibly forge our lives. Brooks Rexroat richly understands how place deeply influences who we are, and these twelve stories are poignant missives that illustrate the ways in which the Midwest is anything but flyover country."

- Anne Valente, author of Our Hearts Will Burn Us Down

"A poignant portrayal of working-class America, of people trudging through the decaying landscape they inherited from their parents, looking for something to latch onto, something or someone to love, some way to live."

- Daniel Abbott, author of The Concrete

"Brooks Rexroat is at his best in *Thrift Store Coats*. These characters have grit and guts, and Rexroat exposes their vulnerabilities as he unravels layers of Midwestern identity. It's an ambitious collection threaded by class and poverty, love lost and found, and the pursuit and failing of the American Dream. The people and places will haunt you as you question your own place in our country's changing landscape."

- Melissa Scholes Young, author of Flood: A Novel

"A collection of savvy, world-weary tales winding through the Midwest valley, Brooks Rexroat's *Thrift Store Coats* takes in an unsentimental yet meticulous panorama stretching from Lake Erie to the Ohio River and beyond, capturing the occasional grace of its people being comforted by those familiar disappointments marking their home when not being assailed by them in the meanwhile. In a landscape dotted with shuttered mills, small-town high school football games, forlorn dive bars and Sunday services, Rexroat skillfully delivers these characters out from obscure plainness and into their own becoming, those who are wandering but never completely lost unto themselves."

- Forrest Roth, author of Gary Oldman is a Building You Must Walk Through

"The stories in Rexroat's *Thrift Store Coats* are full of the hardscrabble, those living on the fringe. And yet, what is too easily cast prosaic, here is painted with crackling humanity, characters searching for meaning in a world rushing by, forgotten and trying to hang on, looking, always looking, toward some future they may never know. A striking collection."

- Robert James Russell, author of *Mesilla* and *Sea of Trees*

"Brooks Rexroat's midwest is a place haunted by repurposed and abandoned warehouses, crumbling infrastructures, and long-silent smokestacks standing like gothic tombs—a kind of small-town Twilight Zone where something used to be but isn't anymore, where everyone knows everyone else but wishes they didn't. (More terrifying, it's also a land of sprawling Megachurches, mall kiosks, pumpkin spice coffees, and invading Dollar Generals). The characters might be stuck in endless cycles of economic bust, burdened memories, and deferred dreams, but it's ultimately the reader who gets caught in *Thrift Store Coats'* gravitational pull. Once you're in, it's near-impossible to leave, and even harder to forget."

- Joseph Bates, author of *Tomorrowland: Stories*

"In *Thrift Store Coats*, Brooks Rexroat evokes an authentic sense of place in each story. From rusted steel in rural Ohio to a dilapidated dock off the Great Lakes, this collection embodies a Midwestern landscape that allows readers to roam 'the gut of this country' in hopes of 'salvaging half-dead things.' Just like the Midwest, these stories are both unrelenting and unforgettable."

- Rob Parrish, author

"The stories in *Thrift Store Coats* are a fusion of heart and grit, adventure and adversity. Here, Brooks Rexroat flexes his literary powers sentence by sentence and establishes himself as a vital voice from the Rust Belt. *Thrift Store Coats* is an electrifying debut from a writer with a shrewd intellect, compiling complex stories of a changing America."

- Angela Palm, author of *Riverine: A Memoir from Anywhere but Here*

thrift store coats

stories by ~~brooks rexroat~~

stories

For Marilyn and Kate and Dan and George and Beth and Jacinda and all the other teachers who both encouraged and demanded—in careful measure.

blood off rusted steel

It's awful as hell to see lights off in the distance and know without hesitation that they're coming for someone with your surname. Instead of heading straight down Birch Pond Road, I took a left onto the state route because lights moving that fast toward his place meant school would be cancelled without question. I wondered instantly what it was he'd done this time, which of those poor creatures had got loose. Figured I ought to go over and see what the damage was this time.

I took the turns too hard that morning, my old Ford swaying side-to-side as I fumed about how uncle James had found one more way to make things difficult, one more way to impose himself on the rest of us. I turned the radio to something fast and loud, cranked it up to keep from thinking hateful things.

I was steamed, too, as I drove, because we had a game that night against Clear Valley. That one had been circled on my calendar for months. The Fighting Salmon hadn't won a game in two years, so it was almost dead certain I'd finally get onto the court. My shoulders were sore because coach even let me practice with the first team instead of playing dummy defense like I had every practice for the past three years. Then I came home and popped foul shots in the driveway until dinner was ready, bundled up in three layers of sweatshirt because this was my chance to impress Dacie Lindt in front of an actual crowd. Thanks to James, that chance was dead.

I had it all planned out in my mind: I would nail a few pretty shots, enjoy the concept of having some sweat from my own palm involved in the handshake line, then clean up in the locker room and bolt toward the cafeteria and the post-game dance where Dacie would stand at the center of a crowd, still wearing her pleated orange and black skirt, like we'd all forget she was a cheerleader if she changed into a dress like everyone else. Later in life, it occurred to me maybe she simply didn't have a dress to change into, but that night, I couldn't have cared less. I was going to walk right up to her in the middle of her peacock routine, not even try to be subtle about it or wait until she stood alone by the drinking fountain or something. I would walk up, smile, and ask her out. I didn't bother to daydream her portion of it—the result was her business. But I knew my part and I was ready.

Of course, whenever school got cancelled, whether it was for snow or flooding or a problem with the boiler or one of my uncle's shenanigans, it meant extra-curriculars were cancelled. Which meant basketball games were cancelled. And meaningless three-pointers at the buzzer. And dances. And daydreams.

When I pulled around the bend and saw all those cruisers, all those camera crews, saw the distant pinpricks of light coming from the ends of shotguns, my gut curled up into a ball.

I squeezed the steering wheel as hard as I could. Again and again the flashes came, each followed by a sharp crack, loud enough for me to hear even before I turned down the stereo. Some came in isolation, others in the small bursts of an automatic. Each flick, I knew, had to be another one of those poor creatures catching its end. The first one I saw was right at the edge of the property, before I even got the truck stopped. A Bengal tiger, endangered as hell, and there he was with his head in the ditchwater and a dozen red pockmarks staining his belly and sides. I swallowed back a gag then took a deep breath to pull myself together. The guns were still popping.

Sheriff Martin stood in the middle of the road with his hands waving, motioning me to pull over. Even in that small of a town, most people my age only knew the look of him from his reelection posters, except for maybe the real serious delinquents. I brought the truck to a stop and he came to my window, pointed a flashlight at me. "Morning, Davis," he said. "You can pull on through, but I have to tell you it's awful ugly. Your aunt's over by the first barn with some of your folks. You need to go see them first, you understand?"

"It's not just the animals, is it?"

"Like I said, son. You need to go on and speak with your kin."

I parked between two of the satellite trucks. Their diesel fumes stung my nose. Before long I'd be wishing for such mildness to come back. The sides of the trucks had the familiar logos of Columbus Stations, but then I saw the Pittsburgh ones and one from Cleveland, a couple of others without insignia, which was a new development. In all, dozens lined the road. An escaped bear or two usually fetched just the local newspaper and a couple of cops—nearly all of them guys I knew from school, a few of them even classmates of mine who dropped out and took the GED early so they could get on with becoming a cop before someone else beat them to the open job. If a person didn't make the force and wanted to stay in town the best options were trash collector, fry cook, or car salesman. So, being a cop was the dream gig for most of us: walk around with a loaded gun and a uniform, look tough and put-together, and take some occasional target practice in the direction of my crazy uncle's animal herd. Maybe even get a color picture in the weekly paper standing hero-like over a lion or two.

That day, they all got their pictures taken. And even though they tried to act later like it had been a solemn and regrettable occasion, I knew better. Those boys made like they were on safari that night and blew away everything they could, whether or not their target was dangerous. All those animals were just deer-in-season for them, and Sheriff Martin was handing out the licenses. They hit everything that moved. A couple rabbits, a squirrel, even Aunt Linda's cat. That morning, all those boy-deputies got their moment of glory, got a big story to exaggerate for their eventual grandkids and color photo newspaper clippings to validate it, the same way their dads and uncles did about Nam or Iraq. I can just picture one of them retelling the story to some dumb kids, turning a sweet-tempered tabby named Princess into a vicious panther, coiled and ready to murder with its six-inch teeth. When the kids would ask for proof, there would be a made-up excuse about a fire that lapped up all the newspapers—anything to keep the lie going. If there's one thing we're good at making around here, it's bigger selves.

Before I reached the barn where my family had gathered, I saw mixed in with the cop cars and ambulances a black sedan with white letters on the side: County Coroner. I decided to skip the chat with Aunt Linda, decided I'd seen enough of the whole mess. I got back in my truck and drove fast, those little flashes chasing me in the rearview the whole way home.

•

The professionals evacuated first and seamlessly: they put their trucks into gear as soon as they could and hit the interstate. Sure, the cameras hung around for a few days, soaking up every last drop of blood they could get away with broadcasting. The reporters with their thick make-up got real practiced at saying the word *tragedy* and talking about how *this small Ohio community will be forever changed*, as if they knew a damn thing about what it was like before. They should've asked me. Instead of wilting on cue and dishing out clichés like all the bewildered-acting neighbors, I would've just said the truth: this place is and always has been absurd, whether it's dead animals or live people. Nothing's ever going to change that. Nothing.

When the humane society people came in a day later, they shook their heads and said lots of versions of *Oh, how terrible*, but couldn't figure out anything productive to do. In the end, their best guess was to spray paint a big black X on each bloated body to prove the animals were actually deceased, then they tacked an embossed and signed license on Aunt Linda's front door that showed we had permission to bury the bodies. With that feeble attempt in the books, they packed up and high-tailed it, too.

The county engineer's office sent out a couple men and a backhoe to dig a pit, and the state Environmental Protection Agency showed up long enough to line the pit with thick black plastic so the decomposing tigers didn't screw up anyone else's drinking water. Then, the important people left with their equipment and their rules, the job half finished.

4

"I'm afraid you'll have to take it from here," one of the EPA workers told Aunt Linda, who nodded and proceeded with evacuating into her house. Everyone else in the family claimed they were busy preparing for his funeral—an event the rest of the town was thinking up interesting reasons to avoid. Dad said what it really came down to was that everyone was more worked up over how to control the cemetery if protestors showed up than they were over proper grieving. My folks would've helped out, I suppose, if I'd really pushed it. But they were three weeks behind getting ready for spring planting on our own farm, and I wasn't about to beg them away from that.

I asked a couple guys from the team, and in the cafeteria they thought the animal burying project sounded cool—but I guess once they told their parents where they were going it all got shot down, because no one actually showed and there I was, left alone with the mess. One more time, I proved to be the least skilled at evacuating, which has always felt like a theme around here. In the end it was just me and a shovel, some lime dust, a saw, a straw baling hook, and my poor old truck.

It stinks like hell burying the week-old corpse of a monkey, a leopard, a bear, a tabby, a horse, each of which has its own tint of rotten. When the sun thaws a six-acre killing field, it's the embodiment of foul. Of course, the smell wasn't even the worst of it. Let's just say animals of that size can't be moved in one piece. My palms ached from friction with rusted tools, and the lime dust tickled my throat into a thousand coughs, which then turned it raw, which made the lime sting like the devil. By the third day of work, I could pick apart whether I was near a big cat or a monkey before I even looked.

•

It's irritating as hell when everyone has just one thing they want to say to you, and it's the one thing you wish you never had to hear again. Take Billy Thiggens, the youngest of the cops out there that night. He was in my math class all the way through school (even though he was supposed to be two years ahead of me and somehow managed to graduate on time). In the day-to-day of it, Billy strikes me as the sort who would cower in a corner if a white bunny rabbit got too rambunctious within five yards of him. But he was one of the first on the scene that night, and to hear him tell it around town he was fierce as Rambo out there. He may well have been, too: with those night-vision goggles on, it must've seemed like one big, hilarious video game.

In class he'd been an okay guy—a little goofy, but the type you'd be okay talking with now and then if you passed each other on the sidewalk or something. Now, though, if I run across him at the gas station or the Subway, all he ever does to try and start a conversation is shape his hand into a fake pistol and point it at me, then wink. I guess it's his moment of glory and I should let him live it. But what really irks me is this: just about everyone else at least has the level of decency to start off their recollection with something about how awful it had been, how sad that the man unlatched each and every one of those cages before he turned a gun on himself, and for no good reason—just plain awfulness. Everybody's got their guess on why he did it, of course, from CNN to the shopping cart jockeys at IGA. Mental disturbance and visions for the Lord and such, but I know the truth: he was just mean. But no one ever asked. They all wanted to tell their own position, or just point a finger-gun like Billy, sucking up all that misery and with some weird internal chemistry turn themselves into sages and heroes. Now, every time Billy points that stupid boney index finger my direction, I want to snap it at the first digit. I want to see what kind of a hero he turns into then. Instead, I've gotten good and practiced at nodding and giving a fat, fake smile that says, "Yeah, man, you're real clever, and I'm just going to keep smiling so you don't follow me around looking for excuses to write me a ticket."

I'll give my teachers credit for at least trying harder than Billy, but in the end the result wasn't much better: they wrote "OK" next to answers that were clearly wrong so my tests got bumped up to an undeserved letter. They accidentally left my tardy mornings off the attendance ledger, too, and it was hard work, not taking advantage of that grace.

"Let me know if there's anything I can do for you," Miss Henderson said in passing at least once a week. She said this because she was a freshman science teacher whose ability to help me was years in the past, and there was absolutely nothing I could ask her for. Coach Thornton didn't give me any playing time, but he took to patting my shoulder a lot at practice, which quickly felt weird in every way.

Mr. Anderson, the guidance counselor, pretended to check his watch every time he passed me in the hall. I guess he was afraid that if we ever made eye contact, I'd ask him for an appointment so I could spill my guts and ask for his expert advice. Thing is: I've never seen the man actually wear a watch. At some level, I wanted to show up in his doorway and watch his face grow pale before bailing him out by asking to talk about colleges, but that would've been no better than Billy's gun.

These were the people in charge of my future, which was depressing enough before the massacre and damning after it.

•

It's hard as hell to scrub blood off the rusted steel of an eighty-four Ford pickup. I know: it sounds useless, scrubbing blood off rust. One of them's no better than the other, at first glance, and it felt oddly like I was developing a useful life skill, sorting out how to differentiate the two. I probably would've left it there, except for that one spot, that one splatter on the top of the left sidewall, positioned just so that I couldn't help staring right at it every time I looked in the rearview mirror, as if the crazy kook and all his animal mess was chasing me around. As much as the incident was tattooed all over everyone's interactions with me, I didn't want it *actually* following me, especially that weekend. And so I scrubbed at that truck, scrubbed until my shoulder and elbow were numb, tried to rid myself of every trace of it. Tried to make the truck as normal as possible, tried to make myself normal.

By the time things calmed down, I lost my shot with Dacie. They never rescheduled the game—both teams were so bad the outcome didn't really matter to anyone. Consequently, I never made it off the bench, never had my moment of glory except the last home game when all the seniors got to start, and then as soon as somebody caught the tip-off, coach wasted a time-out and people clapped and our parents took pictures while we senior benchwarmers trotted back to our rightful places and the marginally more skillful sophomores took back the court for the remainder of the game.

Even if that moment had produced equal parts glory as it had embarrassment (at least Mom let it rest with the camera, once I took a seat and put my nylon pullover back on), it wouldn't have been worthwhile to bother with Dacie. By then, she was already seeing one of the senior wrestlers, a squat little muscle-bound guy named Logan whose senior year was just a big countdown to the army. I guess Dacie had her sights on escaping town and seeing the world one base at a time, so she latched onto him hard and it quickly got the look of something permanent with hand-holding in the hallways and the gifting of various stuffed animals and chocolates. I was busted up about it for a couple days after the news spread around school, but that's the sort of thing you can't let weigh you down too long. In a town this size, if you don't go off to college or find someone to marry by the end of high school, chances are you'll have to wait a good four or five years before the first round of divorces kick in.

So I took after Abbie Greenway. She wasn't blond with big, pouty lips like Dacie, but she had cute brunette ringlets and she was the sort of kind girl you can see yourself getting along with for a good long while, the sort you don't imagine ever having to pick up from the bar at two in the morning because she's taken off all her clothes again and started swinging her stiletto heels at the bouncer.

I pressed and scrubbed with Brillo and Scotch-Brite pads and torn-up T-shirts and even a little heel of sponge. I tried solvents and detergents and vinegar and that orange smelling stuff with the little pieces of lava rock in it—I tried everything I could to separate blood from metal and remove the stain from my view, to put it as far out of sight as all those poor decaying beasts. I scrubbed until my shoulder and elbow went numb, then I switched arms and scrubbed some more until Mom came out and shouted "Shouldn't you be getting ready?" and I looked up to see half the sun had already slipped below the horizon.

It was time to shower, to clean myself instead of the truck. I stopped before I pulled open the screen door, though, and looked at the deepening tone of the sky, a sky that within the course of moments had turned itself from clear and pristine to deep and foreboding red. Like rust, like blood. The things that surrounded me were encapsulated in that sky. For a moment, I considered calling Abbie Greenway and thinking up the kindest way to tell her to forget it. But I did what I do—what we do around here—I shrugged it off and pushed forward, showered and dressed, and looked around the basement for an umbrella big enough to shade a pair. I picked up her corsage from the Kroger on the way to her place, even bought a couple of sodas while I was there, since I figured we'd be facing a solid wait once we got at the Olive Garden.

I waited for Abbie to say something about the truck, about how clean it was maybe, but I guess it was too dark by then for her to even notice. As we drove and the drops started to fall heavier and the wipers started to swish she just wanted to know things like what sorts of problems I thought might be on the geometry test and where we might work once school was finished for good.

She didn't ask me why we took the roundabout way to the prom—the three-mile detour that had become habit for me during the previous three months. Abbie just kept up the conversation through the ride and through dinner. On the last stretch before we got to the school she reached her left hand across the console and held onto mine. The purple-dyed carnations that circled her wrist tickled my right arm and I told her it felt nice. We reached the parking lot, full already of SUVs and pickups and a couple of rented limousines. After the dance was over, there would be new and important things to consider, large things not easily undone. But for a moment we sat quietly, said and did nothing.

It's comforting as hell to sit next to someone who can ignore what your last name means to the rest of town. Who doesn't see the difference between blood and rusted steel. I peeked briefly into the rearview and saw nothing important.

"Ready?" she asked.

I nodded and got out to open her door, to help her down onto the damp asphalt in those precarious heels of hers. I lifted the umbrella over her head and as we walked past the truck bed and toward the doors of the gymnasium, all I saw was rust.

angel of death

When the phone rings at half past one in the morning, Lewis doesn't fumble for the receiver. His arm arcs straight for it, habit-laden and well practiced.

"Who is it tonight?" he asks, and flips on the bedside lamp while he listens for the name. "I'll be right there."

Lewis exhales, drops the phone back onto its plastic cradle, and pushes himself up off the mattress. He hobbles toward the clothes he's left draped over a chair beside his bedroom door. He slips them on as quickly as he can manage, checks himself in the bathroom mirror to make sure he's gotten each shirt button through its proper hole. He cups his hands to splash cool water on his face, and walks to the kitchen. In the stillness of young morning, the only sound is the clack-clump of his own gait, his feet striking heavy and heavier on the ancient wood floors of a home his father built by hand.

It's a drive of three and-a-half miles to the East Ohio Veterans' Home. Lewis feels the drooping of his heavy head and eyelids. He's aware of his slumping shoulders. It was a hard day already with a skipped lunch (the Tupperware sandwich box still waiting in the break room refrigerator), two extra hours of paperwork, and late afternoon conferences that simply couldn't be pushed off to another day. With great difficulty, he'd finally gotten himself to sleep, a solid two hours later than his typical bedtime of nine.

His blood pressure is up lately, his stress levels palpable from too much work, too many late night calls. It's been the coldest winter in a decade and even on the weeks the paycheck gets cut on time, it's too often a coin flip between heating oil and meal money. But the worst of it is the quiet, the way he's hardly spoken to a soul outside of work duties and his Sunday and Wednesday trips to First Baptist of St. Clairesville. Even those church trips have become sad, as the lists of illness and condolence published in the weekly bulletin grow longer while the aging congregation grows steadily smaller.

But this is his chosen job, his chance to serve those who did what he could not, all those years ago when one irregular tick in his own heart kept him from knowing firsthand the many horrors other men recite to him daily. When the phone rings, there is no ignoring it. There is no point in pondering excuses.

He yawns and pauses at the electric coffeemaker in the kitchen. He looks up at the big clock over the stove and the way it just doesn't stop. He hopes the caffeine is just a want, because that second hand is not worth fighting. It'll win, every time. On his way out the door, he picks up a weathered old Bible, bound in leather and marked in the most important spots by small slips of paper.

The air bites at his coarse skin. He shivers, and then shuffles along the walkway, careful to bring his feet straight up and straight down so he doesn't slip on any ice. If there's one thing he doesn't need tonight, it's another fall. He was out of commission for a week after the last one, the doctor at the public hospital refusing to let him get back to work until he'd passed a battery of tests.

He wipes half an inch of powdery snow from the front and rear windshields of his old sky blue Buick, slips into the driver's seat, turns the key, and shifts into gear without letting the vehicle's engine properly warm itself. He hates doing this; someday the car will give out for good, and he'll have no one to blame but himself. More importantly, he'll have no way to get to work.

He eases backward, turns out of his driveway onto the county throughway. The car continues to move after he depresses the break fully, and he can only wait, hope the thing stops before gliding off the road. Just shy of his own mailbox, the car finally rests, and he grips the icy steering wheel tight, pushes the gas pedal as hard as he dares at this hour, in this weather.

It's quarter to two, and the bar between his house and the veterans' home will clear out any moment, his drunken neighbors pouring onto the already perilous roads. He does what they told him at the Elkton Seniors Center and watches the white line when someone comes his way with their bright lamps on. That reflective strip on the road's edge helps him steer when he can't see anything else, blinded by oncoming brightness. He hopes, and even whispers a small prayer each time a car comes his way, that the other driver will manage to stay on the far side of the road, and that by focusing on the white stripe, Lewis will manage to stay on his own.

He wonders, though, as he stares hard away from what seems to be the particularly bright lamps of a pickup truck, if this is what it feels like to be one of his clients in those last seconds: something overwhelming and bright taking over every sense until there's nothing real left around them. He wonders how it really feels to encounter the moment through which he's held so many hands, the moment over which he's about to preside once more. In this instant, he wants to look up, to know what it's like, all that enveloping white.

But that would be selfish, he tells himself once again. Too many others count on him, so he fixates on the side of the road until the lamps have passed, and the going is safe. He nudges the gas pedal just a touch farther and out of habit checks the dashboard clock, even though it's been stuck on four-seventeen in the afternoon for nearly a decade.

•

Lewis nods at Jacob, the night watchman. He smiles at Marcy, the evening receptionist who spends most of her shift reading romance novels, still labeled with orange price tags from the thrift store. He returns a wave from Bernie, the custodian, who never stops swaying that big heavy mop even as he lifts his hand to acknowledge Lewis. Everyone is friendly but no one speaks: with so many weak and weary hearts in the building, there's no need to say the chaplain's name out loud after hours.

Lewis walks the beige hallway tile as softly as he can manage but there is no hiding a late-night arrival from even the weariest old ears. They recognize his gait. It pulls them from sleep, and because of that he hates his limp, the click-clack tapping of the feet that support an overly thick stomach, a broken-down frame, an artificial knee. He curses himself, curses his ailment on their behalf. Then he whispers a prayer, asking forgiveness for the curse. It's a spiral of difficulty, always trying to stay on the right side of life.

The men will all be wondering one cold thing: *who this time.* He tries so hard to make his thick rubber soles press more softly against the floor, but it does no good at all. It never has. He feels the men watch through their cracked doorways as he struggles onward. Lewis stops at the chapel and pokes his head in. Sometimes, the men want to spend their final minutes in that room—by far the least dismal place in the vast complex, softened by wood walls and an arched ceiling, fake stained glass behind the altar, a few oil paintings of a smiling Christ. But the chapel is empty so he walks back into the sterile, florescent white of the hallway and walks to room one hundred seventeen, the one occupied by Stewart Walters. He pauses outside the door, breathes deep, composes himself. He whispers, "Help me do well for him, Lord," and then steps through the doorframe, hoping he's not too late.

●

Stewart's eyes are barely open. Adrienne, the new night nurse, stands on the other side of his bed, along with the superintendent and the night doctor.

The doctor taps the face of his watch with a finger, just once—the signal that it'll just be moments now. Lewis nods, glad he skipped that coffee. He forces a moderate smile onto his face.

"Stewart, friend, it's very good to see you this evening." His tone is warm, soft, measured. Rehearsed, in the precise tones taught so long ago in seminary. Lewis reaches down and gently squeezes Stewart's hand, which is cold and slowly trembles. Sometimes the men can't hear Lewis or even see him by this point. He watches Stewart's eyes, and finds some small hint of recognition, a tiny dilation. He's still lucid then, at least partially.

"I'd love to read to you from the Lord's word tonight, if you'd like that. Is there a story you'd like to hear?"

Stewart nods slightly, but when he tries to move his mouth, nothing happens except a soundless budging of his dry and deeply ridged lips. The nurse, Adrienne, picks up a manila file folder and passes it to Lewis. On the second page, underneath the contact information for next of kin, is a favorite Bible verse, the twenty-third Psalm. Lewis smiles against his internal impulse. He hates reading this at the end, hates reminding dying men about green pastures and shadows of death because part of it is so near and the other so uncertain. He's read it at bedsides and memorials and vigils and has written it on cards of condolence. If he had his way, it would be stricken from the good book altogether on a blended basis of sadness and absurdity. But this is Stewart's choice, written months ago in his own shaking hand, and Lewis will oblige.

"Would you like to pray with me first?" Lewis asks.

Stewart slightly lifts his free hand and points to the Bible. He always was one to listen, to learn quietly from others. In the dining hall and at the card tables, during bingo, on outings to the village park—the others would talk and share their tales of glory. Stewart, he would urge them on, compel them for detail, but of all the men who'd ever passed through the building, Lewis had never once heard Stewart offer a battle tale. That was a bond they shared, Lewis and Stewart. Now the task of listening will fall just to the man who claims it as a vocation. This will be a fitting close: Stewart resting as someone regales him onward. Lewis shuts his eyes for the quickest of instants to ask for a calm and painless end to Stewart's life.

The chaplain opens his worn Bible and begins to read, though he knows the full chapter and most of its neighbors by heart. The men are more comfortable when he appears to be reading, rather than reciting to them. There is warmth in the charade, and so he pretends to read words that have long lost the power of their meaning. After a few words, he looks up and sees the tinge of a smile falling over Stewart's face. The frail man closes his eyes. His chest rises slowly and pauses before his lungs release the air so that each breath seems, for the slimmest instant, to have been the last.

Lewis returns to the page. Maybe he is fooling himself. Maybe he doesn't pretend at reading to make the men feel better, but to avoid watching their final instant. So he can see them near death and after it, but never *during*. He stares at the little black letters on onionskin pages—too small even though it's a bulky large-print edition—and reads the rest of the chapter. He starts in on the twenty-fourth. He is aware of movement across the room, across the bed, the doctor and the nurse moving and checking, measuring, marking, noting. One hand still wrapped around Stewart's cool fingers and the other supporting the Bible, Lewis reads on and on, ignoring what's happening in the room, ignoring the quickness, the beeping machinery, the motion, the rustling of fabrics, the leaning and dipping and whispering. Lewis reads the word of the Lord, the comforting word, the good word, until he feels a firm hand grasping his shoulder.

"He's gone," the superintendent says. "He's gone."

Lewis squeezes once more on the limp hand of a man who won medals and praise for the way he fought and killed his way across Europe, but who never wanted to talk of anything but those around him, the family he loved, the friends, the obnoxious dog he once raised, the neighbors he kept in this stark building. As the nurse disconnects tubes and cables from the body, Lewis ponders this: the way a man's life can be defined by the instant when he was asked to fight, rather than the years he chose to love. He takes a ballpoint pen from the pocket of his trousers and marks this thought down in the margins of his Bible, in case it might be meaningful in some future memorial service. Maybe in Stewart's, if he's asked to deliver it.

The superintendent calls for a transport to the coroner, which will wind up being whichever commercial ambulance service is closest at the moment. Sometimes, there's an argument in the lobby if two competing drivers arrive too close together, but at least it's happened late enough tonight to avoid any of that nonsense. No one working this shift cares enough to fight. Lewis takes up the folder to check on family records: a daughter and two adult grandchildren in Arizona, a third in California. He wonders whether he ought to call them now, or wait until the morning.

"You look tired," Adrienne says. "Go home. We'll make the call."

"No," he says. He regrets how firm it comes out. "That's my job."

She shrugs and opens a steel cabinet at the foot of the bed. She pulls a plastic wrapper containing a flag off the top of a pile. "Give me a hand with this?" she asks. Lewis helps to drape it over the body. The superintendent's cell phone buzzes once, and he reads the message. "Transport's here," he says. "Quick tonight, at least."

The three of them lift the flag-covered body onto a steel gurney that Adrienne fetches from a storage room. Lewis leads them out into the hallway. There, standing outside their doors, are the men of the East Ohio Veterans' Home. Some lean on canes or walkers, some stand straight and tall on their own power, some lean against the doorway, but each holds his right hand crisply against the temple in salute. Lewis leads the gurney through the building, toward the receiving bay. Some of the saluting men's eyes are damp with tears. Others smile, recognizing that their friend's acute pain is done. They whisper kind words as the body passes, wishing well their brother.

•

Lewis picks up the phone and dials the daughter first but gets no answer. The first granddaughter doesn't pick up either, but the Arizona grandson does.

"Can I help you," he says tersely, as if he doesn't particularly mean for it to be a question.

"This is brother Lewis at the East Ohio Veterans Home, and I've called to offer my condolences—"

"I see," the man says. There's a pause, long enough that Lewis almost speaks up to make sure the line hasn't gone dead. When the voice returns, there's a hush to it, but no sadness. "We thought he was going to hang on to the end of time. What do we need to do? Where should my wife send the card?"

"If you'll call the home first thing in the morning, they'll walk you through those details. I want you to know that if you need any counseling, I'm more than happy to help you through the grieving process. I'll just give you my number—"

The dial tone returns at the other end. Lewis sighs and hangs up. He stops by the dining room to see if any coffee remains. Just a little left, and barely warm. He takes a third of a foam cup and downs it, just enough of a swig to keep him awake on the trip home, and not an instant longer, he hopes. He wipes his lips, pitches the cup, and turns—his pivot encompasses three shuffling steps before he can begin hobbling forward, past the lobby, past Jacob, who pats Lewis on the back and past Marcy, who's put down her book and taken up paperwork and past Bernie, still sweeping, whose head ducks just fractions lower this time as he nods.

He encounters no opposing headlamps during the drive, everyone else in bed for the night. Lewis cranks the key to his front door and walks into the empty home. He strips off his clothes and drapes them over the chair again—just in case—and then shrugs into his bathrobe and slips into bed, pulls the heavy blanket tight against his chin. He regrets the coffee as he clinches his eyes and lays awake, tired but with blood pumping too quick now to allow sleep. He wonders, as he rests quiet, still, thoroughly alone, whether anyone will be there to read him away, to pray with him, to ask him his favorite verse—or whether some anonymous pastor will passively recite the twenty-third Psalm before hired and anonymous hands shovel the loose ground back into place. Whether his grandchildren will weep or shrug. Whether the calls will be made immediately, or whether the dialer will wait until after morning's strong, black coffee. In the middle of all that three o'clock darkness, he wonders how very bright the lights will be for him, and how soon they will come. He wonders whether anyone will remember him at all since he has only been God's reluctant soldier and never man's.

thrift store coats

They put thirty of us in line by order of last name that day, like we were going for grade school class photos instead of termination papers. Since our last names were the same by then, they put Mary first by a fraction of an *M*. We would bounce back, I thought. What else *could* we do? I looked at Mary—clearly, she wasn't thinking the same thing. She was about to punch someone's face. Out in the cube farm, our friends and neighbors and drinking buddies who'd staved off the line stared at their screens, typing like nothing had changed.

Every day, we'd read wire reports about how the Internet was slaughtering the newspaper industry, how foreign manufacturing was killing our town's chances at a comeback, how big-box stores were strangling Main Street—ours and everyone else's. With all that murder in our vicinity, we'd known what was coming. But when it actually went down, the mess came hard and sudden.

The walls were so thin we heard every word of the spiel each employee got. When our turn came, we had the speech memorized. We tried to go in together, but the freaking mustachioed rent-a-cop they brought in for the occasion wasn't having it, so Mary walked in alone. She mouthed along with the publisher as he fired her. Halfway through, he stopped and shouted, "You think we enjoy this?" That's what it finally took for anyone to look up from a screen.

Everyone on the floor waited for her to lay in Hurricane Mary style, but she said nothing. A few seconds later, his voice raised again: "All right, just go." I hugged her before I went in. I didn't even sit when he pointed to the chair, just held out my hand and said, "Give me the damn papers." He did, and I took my wife out of that place, drove her straight home where we drank ourselves stupid with everything left in the fridge. We cried, then we yelled, we had manic sex and cried some more and yelled once more from sheer habit. In the morning, I brewed coffee to help us fight our headaches. The grounds were the last from a brown paper bag of artisanally roasted beans from a shop in Akron. As the percolator started letting loose that wonderful scent, all I could think of was that this was a full-stop on comfort, that we were heading right back to a world of freeze-dried, generic crap. I was aware, as I thought this, that my father would've smacked me across the face for letting that spoiled-brat idea even run a lap around my head. He'd have told me to buck up and get on with it, but the coffee smelled so amazing, and all our nice things were about to go out the window that it was impossible not to pout for at least a tick.

At some level, Mary must've felt the same way, because it took us half an eternity to drink that coffee, as we sat mostly silent across the table from each other.

We were about an hour in (surrounded by boxes of clothes we'd decided to donate instead of lugging along) when she decided it would be comforting to say, "It'll be alright, I swear. Just like it was in Portland." It took me three laps around the block before I calmed down. I walked back in the door and up the stairs and went back to sorting without saying a word. You get real good at quiet seething when you marry up.

•

Whenever I told an advisor or professor I planned to work in newspapers, they raised their eyebrows, as if I'd just told them I planned on being a rock drummer or linebacker or a leprechaun. Then came a pejorative tap on the shoulder and a speech about how mean things were out there, as if I didn't already know. As if I didn't grow up across the street from the ruins of three factories and a mill, the hollow innards of all the grown-ups' former jobs. As if I grew up with some idealistic daydreams about how everything was going to be okay. This was absolute garbage and I tried to tell them but they crossed their knees and sighed a lot and pretended to look at test scores they didn't have on hand. They passed on their wisdom, real good and firm. In halting, professorly phrases, they told me all the things I was smart enough to do instead: computer programmer and data analyst and parole officer and arts management professional (whatever that is).

Dad, though, he was more insightful about my announcement. After he made it clear and expletive-laden that this choice meant a kiss of poverty, he nodded and sank into his armchair. He sipped whatever remedy was in his glass that day—we'll go with bourbon based solely on the percentages—and said, "It makes sense."

Shocked at the general lack of shouting in his response, I pushed for clarification. "Yeah?"

"You grow up in the gut of this country, you get practice salvaging half-dead things." I wasn't sure I agreed, but I nodded vigorously, having braced for a knock-down-drag-out that, if poorly executed on my part, would've put me on a pre-law track, ripe for a graceless, fast plunge into bagboy status. "We try and turn dead factories into shopping malls, warehouses into apartments. We leave rusting cars in our lawns, collect barns full of useless crap. Comes with the territory. We see so much turn rotten, we can't help trying to save the condemned."

That's when the pat on the shoulder finally did come—even *he* couldn't resist it. "Just keep in mind, I won't bail you out. Don't you even ask."

He drank up, set the glass down heavy enough that there was a little ringing sound that floated afterward, searing his proclamation into my head, and that was that.

Mary came from the razor's edge of the east coast and had sensibilities that would've suited the most stiff-lipped of those codger professors: her preservationist instinct largely came with the preface, *self-*. It wasn't her fault: she grew up in places where things grew green and upright, where dried-up things didn't sit around for ages—it got bulldozed or pitched and replaced and made pretty again. After northeastern boarding schools and an apparently robust six years of undergraduate college in New

York, Mary lived in Portland, Oregon for a year. She used to throw that particular fact nonchalantly into conversations, as if I could forget it. She and two friends squatted in an abandoned appliance warehouse—just walked in one day and found the water still running, the electric still hooked up—and that's where they stayed. They furnished it by 'salvaging' dumpsters and haggling for second-hand furniture at yard sales and flea markets just like so many of my friends had growing up. To them, though, it was a game. They painted the walls with graffiti, climbed in and out through the fire escape like it was their front door. (I've always wondered who paid the electric for that building, and why no one noticed the usage spike, but I never asked—didn't want the story to keep going.)

They took quirky cash jobs like picking apples or handing out furniture store flyers. Mary once stood outside a check-cashing place in a Statue of Liberty costume all day. When the manager came to collect the costume at closing time, there was significant confusion stemming from the fact that Mary hadn't been hired but simply walked by, thought it looked fun, and told some pimple-faced teenager to give her the cape and take a day off. By conversation's end, the boss gave her fifty bucks to leave and never come back. With their odd job money, the girls bought gaudy clothes from run-down thrift shops. *To be ironic*, she told me when I asked why, then she elaborated that gentrified vintage stores were off limits. They scoured bins in the seediest pockets of town, played dress-up in other people's discards. Sometimes they ate at soup kitchens.

"What about the people who *needed* it?" I asked.

"We *did*," she said, and shrugged. "Besides, we paid. With empathy."

No one else I've ever met could've said that with a straight face, let alone get anyone to believe them. But Mary could, and she knew it.

A whole year, they did this, with freshly printed bachelor's degrees and jobs waiting. Back then, jobs always seemed to be waiting. *Help Wanted*, everywhere—office buildings and cafes and mall stores.

I used to wonder why she didn't stay out west—another one of those paltry details that clammed her up so quick. Sometimes she would mumble about how it doesn't rain enough here: "What's the sense in so much gloom if you get no water?"

I forced a smile like I thought it was funny, and it might've been, if things were going better. The closest I ever got to an explanation was that she got bored, packed up, and moved to Youngstown. Finger-on-the-map stuff. I gave her my best *you're lying* look, the first time she said it, but she smiled and looked at me with unabated clarity. "That's how it happened."

•

There wasn't any point in staying in Youngstown once we got booted, so we moved to Akron. I clerked at Target and waited tables at Chili's, neither of which went well, financially or otherwise. There were broken dishes, anemic tips, and the unfortunate bobbling of a fifty-pound bag of dog food that left the toy section smelling like tuna for the final week they let me stay. I was good with a pen, I told my manager, who didn't seem sympathetic.

"We'll call you when we hire a store publicist," she said as I handed back my red clerk's apron.

"Really?"

"There's no such thing."

"Oh."

Mary went back to grad school on credit cards. This seemed a good idea at the time. The words *return on investment* came out of both our dumb mouths. Repeatedly. During the second semester, she sold her car. I sold mine during summer session.

Her parents flew in long enough to see her graduate. They took a cab straight to campus, watched her cross the stage, took us to dinner (cringing the whole time, as if our skies had rained fly ash on their food) and raced back to the airport three hours early to make certain they didn't miss their flight.

We packed up that night for a section eight project in Cleveland, bars on even the third floor windows. But the cheaper rent would cut back on our debt, we hoped.

"It'll be an adven—" she tried to say.

"Don't," I said.

Armed with a teaching degree and state certificate, Mary set out to finding inevitable work because everyone talks about teacher shortages and how schools need *good* teachers. She shipped resumes by the crateful. We waited months for responses that contained the phrase *someone else more closely met our needs*. I told her I wished I knew that line when I was dating. She didn't find it close to amusing.

"This," she told me one night over instant coffee and Scrabble, "is why everyone talks about crummy teachers. Good ones can't get work." Then she played a fifty-seven-point word and ruined a move I'd been plotting for twenty minutes.

"You should've thrown your student teaching evaluations. Like the Black Sox in the world series," I said. (Fourteen-point word.)

"That's a sport thing, right?" (Forty-six point word.)

"You should've botched it. Then you'd be a low-price commodity." (Eight-point word.)

"Shame I didn't think of that." (Twenty-nine points.)

"Any chance you'd like to trade for three U's?"

"Not the slightest." (Seven points.)

By the end of the game, we'd culled the *work experience* section from her resume, but then the HR replies were angry. She was a liar, they said, and the simplest Internet search proved she had plenty of work experience and just whom was she trying to fool?

•

She'd already signed a yearlong lease by the time she walked into the newspaper office and told them that she'd like a job and they ought to give her one. They interviewed her on the spot. I was well positioned to see all of this because a month earlier they'd rolled my college internship over to a minimum wage reporting job. I was at my desk fidgeting with a retractable pen (I did this a lot—prewriting, I called it—but I really *was* thinking) when the front door burst open and in walked a tall, thin brunette with a Kinkos folder full of resumes pinned under her arm. She wore bright red lipstick and tortoiseshell glasses and she was about to distribute resumes door-to-door like fliers for a punk rock show, except that she nailed it on the first try. No training, of course, and her diploma read "Personalized General Studies in the Liberal Arts," but in the space of ten minutes, she talked some of the sternest people I've ever met into letting her start from scratch on full salary. Later that week, around the tar-gummed coffee pot, half the reporters in the office whispered some sort of remark about how hot she was, and I didn't argue. But I was far more intrigued by the rest of her. The way the world swept aside for her as she moved. *That* was hot. Pixie cuts were a dime a dozen, even in Youngstown; swagger was interesting, and I swear if God gave her a different body she'd have been a boxing champ.

Ed had just been fired for *inappropriate personal use of company property*, so I wishfully thought maybe she'd get the empty cubicle across from mine. But her tour finished with handshakes and an escort across the room to the features desk. That's when my editor tapped my back and asked if my story was finished.

"Oh—yeah, yeah," I said. "I'm putting it into the folder now." And I did. Except, it *wasn't* done, and this time the copy desk didn't catch (or intentionally ignored) two unfinished sentences right in the middle of the story and a quote with no attribution.

I moved it along into the folder for finished work and gave myself a solid half hour of daydreaming time, camouflaged by some daft notepad doodling. I looked her way, just in case she might catch my eyes and crack a meet-me-at-the-coffee-pot smile, but of course, she didn't give me a second look, so I put down my ambition and went back to work.

The next morning, that train wreck of an unfinished article ran on the front of the business section, and people never learned all they could've about why Meachem's Groceries went belly-up. Of course, readers knew—whether or not the sentences were in ink. They understood the mills closed, investors fled, graduates raced out of town so fast that Greyhound could've placed a velvet-roped queue outside Youngstown High's gym each commencement day. The town had dried up; even the mafia—which at one point ran the place so thoroughly there'd been an entire car lot devoted to the resale of vehicles whose owners had *left town*—packed up and called it quits. About the only people still making a decent go of it seemed to be the hookers, pot dealers, and bookies—the sellers of distraction.

•

I wrote a handful of stories for underground newspapers in Cleveland (most of which turned out to be stapled 'zines) and a couple of blogs. Each *Help Wanted* ad swore up and down that writers would be compensated once the venture turned a profit. None of them came close to lasting that long. On the more legitimate front, I did freelance work for three advertising firms, hoping to jostle myself into line for a full-time gig. But all I ever got were leftovers: half-finished jobs orphaned when staff workers moved on to more vital work. I salvaged assignments and sent them to project managers I'd never met in person using free wireless at cafes. Most of the time, I couldn't afford even a small black coffee, so I sat in the back, tried to slip in and out, unnoticed. One day, I saw a *Help Wanted* sign behind the register at Mug's Cafe. I asked the barista about it, but he laughed and pointed to a binder of resumes on the counter behind him. "Those are from people who actually buy something when they come in," he said. "But seriously. Can I get you something this time?"

"Small coffee, I guess," I said. "Black."

"Figures," he said. For that remark, I skipped my regular two-seat table and plunked my stuff on a four-top, then nursed that coffee for four hours, right through lunch rush.

Mary babysat and walked dogs and didn't hear back about waitress jobs and writing jobs and more teaching jobs. She told me how happy she was, how much this reminded her of the warehouse. Sometimes I laughed, because: what else? Sometimes I bit my lip raw and sometimes I said, "Please…" But every time I approached the point of telling her to *Knock it the hell off because this is not Portland*, I took one look at her and knew that she could be with anyone else on the damn planet and if I wanted to remain married, quiet was going to be crucial. *Portland, Portland, Portland*, I heard, and I imagined her bailing on me for the Peace Corps and falling into the arms of a dashing expatriate Brazilian volunteer or a Luxembourgian prince. *Portland, Portland, Portland.*

She paid for a substitute teacher's license and paid more for a background check, bought CPR lessons, and a first-aid card. She added those expensive lines to her resume while I heated instant soup. She placed our rotary phone on the floor next to her side of the bed so she could grab it if it ever rang at four in the morning with a sub offer.

"Don't worry, honey," she said. "I'll grab it before it wakes you." It never rang, though, and by October, her smile was trending dimmer than the autumn sky. She stopped talking about the northwest. Stopped using words like *humble* and *romantic*. Portland finally fell off the map—but so did her smile, which made my victory hollow.

Each night, we both seemed to move closer to the edges of the bed (the covers, of course, went with her). One morning, I woke to find a wall of pillows between us. I figured, at first, this was an accident, just how we'd budged them around in our sleep. They were back in perfect place the next morning, and I knew there was purpose. I also knew to keep my mouth shut, knew she was on the brink of fleeing for Portland or anyplace else. The third night, I got desperate enough to buy a handful of lottery tickets on the way home from work. The fourth night, I didn't even bother putting the pillows back in place before we slept. I felt like an East Berliner, locked out and alone. I considered spraying graffiti on my side.

Walls went up everywhere, rising in unison with the bills: condiments between us on the table, knitting supplies on the couch. It even seemed like there was a bigger gap between our garments in the closet, as if she didn't want our clothes to touch. We were crumbling under our own weight, and I had no idea how to fix it, so I buried myself in table scrap work, tried to ignore the growing chasm.

A week into the segmentation, I took a long walk to clear my head. The air got crisp; at home on the south end of the state, the leaves were surely turning. In our neighborhood, the greys and tans held fast year-round, disregarding time and season. Truce, I thought as I headed home. Truce, I picked up half-wilted flowers from a corner store. I neared the building, walked between lean yet muscular teenagers who played hooky on our stoop, not concerned enough by me to hide their beers. I looked at them out of the corners of my eyes, the same way they looked at me. I nodded in the slight fashion of someone who doesn't really want to nod but has to. They should be in school, I thought. But then, I should've been at work. I fumbled through my pocket for the three keys I needed then click-clack, click-clack, click-clack—turned three tones of silver and brass until the locks were undone, then shoved my way inside. Click-clack, click-clack, click-clack, I threw all three deadbolts back in place and stepped onto the threadbare stairway carpet.

At the landing, I heard her voice and slowed up, hoping it was someone about a job.

"No, not yet. Not now—I know, but it's not that easy."

I stepped closer.

"Yes, it came, and I appreciate it, but it's not even a dent…No, of course I didn't tell him…It piles up so fast—no, he's not. Don't say that. I mean, I see what you're saying, but…"

I didn't bother stepping softly.

Click-clack, click-clack, click clack, the deadbolts flew open. Back through the teens, I stepped harder on the sidewalk, tossed the flowers in a dumpster. It didn't even feel like autumn anymore—it was just damn cold.

•

Six months after she arrived in Youngstown, she sauntered into one of Ben's parties, thrown in honor of a new copy desk clerk. Ben threw a party every Friday whether or not there was anyone to welcome (Mary skipped her own welcome, and no one even shrugged over it, because the Coors cooler stayed full). She sat alone on a couch, and I went for the vodka before claiming the cushion next to her.

"Business department, right?"

"Breaking news, but yeah. It's almost always a dead business."

"They showed me one of your articles when I first got here."

"Yeah?" I was about to puff my chest.

"You're the cautionary tale. Ricketts says you're a good reporter, but he handed me back some gibberish piece about a grocery store and told me if I didn't proofread, the copy desk would let it through just to make me look like an ass."

"That one's on you," I said.

"Yeah?" She did an Audrey Hepburn with her eyebrows.

I told her about the hour-long tirade I got over that one, about how the discrepancies were filled by my visions of her sundress and the world folding up at her arrival.

She filled her glass from a bottle of cheap whiskey. "So, you hate me, or what?"

"Kind of." It came out a little slurred, and I wished I were as drunk as I probably sounded. "But also, I'm kind of in love."

She put her hand on my knee and I got junior high-level tingles. She kissed my cheek and said, "We better make your failure worthwhile. Where you taking me tomorrow?" I drained my cup and told her it was a surprise.

I took her all the way up to Cleveland Heights for the Second Saturday Gallery Hop because I imagined her as the sort of girl who would enjoy that. I'd never been to one, just read about them. The whole way there I hoped hard against it being terrible. She never said whether she enjoyed it or not, but she did stop at what seemed to be the thousandth place selling handmade coffee mugs and bought a pair. A frizzy-haired man gladly took her money, gave her too much change (which she corrected), and he wrapped each mug in newspaper before handing over a pair of nondescript paper lumps.

On the way out, she handed me one of them. "For the office," she said.

"What made you buy *these*?" I asked when we got out of earshot. She looked at me like I was a little crazy. "I mean, every gallery is selling the same plain brown clay mugs. What set these apart?"

"Why does anything have to be set apart?"

She lifted her nondescript clump of paper and I raised mine and we tapped them together and headed for the car.

On the way home, she reached over and held my right hand on the armrest, then fell asleep in the passenger seat.

I kept a clipping of that god-awful article, stuck it into a shoebox full of photos and high school love letters. I had it framed when we moved in together. That story was the last thing we took off the walls, each time we had to move out.

•

"Let's start a winter garden," she said out of the blue. It was a week after I overheard the phone call, and we still hadn't spoken about it. The garden sounded asinine, and I wanted to say so. But I was terrified to disagree, figuring it would spark the last argument.

The only soil nearby was out back, a tiny, stinking patch in the building's courtyard—land that made Pripyat seem splendidly arable. But it did seem a useful distraction, so she looked up cold-weather crops, wrote out a list and sent me to Big Lots. Each seed package was expired, but nothing would rise from that dirt anyway, so I shrugged and paid in exact pocket change. We used a milk jug to carry water out back. She found a spade and a tiny hoe (two dollars apiece) at a pop-up flea market in a vacant lot by Canal Avenue. Our building's back door was bolted shut, so we used the fire escape to reach the lot. One load at a time, we carried our arsenal of supplies down clanking ladders—neighbors poked their heads out windows like irritated whack-a-moles, telling us to *shut the hell up* and *keep it down for god's sake*.

The ground was littered with junk presumably chucked from neighbors' windows or deposited by wind: torn plastic bags, used rubbers, diapers, broken toys, even a couple of needles. Slowly, we removed the trash and cleared dead grass and rocks from a ten-foot-by-ten-foot plot leaving space on each edge of the lot for a walkway. We probably should've gotten permission, or thought harder about what awful things comprised that soil. Instead we simply went to work. She turned over the ground while I pressed dried-out seeds into slimy clay then watered our crooked rows. We didn't speak that first day, but we didn't throw anything at each other, either. It was a start. She even kissed my cheek while I planted the final yam seeds. A root vegetable, of course, would never grow in that soil (whether or not it was suited to the climate), nor would most of what we'd planted. But we needed to bury them there, needed to try. We looked at each other, smiled slightly, and creaked our way up the ladder.

•

I stopped at the gas station for a soda and candy on my way to the plasma bank. Needles terrify me, and when my turn was up for childhood immunizations, nurses knew before I even walked in to have a Coke and suckers on hand to steady me after I returned from blackout. Inside, I stared at the floor first, but it was covered with stains that correlated suspiciously with the chairs. The faint smell of piss crept through the base atmosphere of tobacco; I stopped looking at the floor, traced the ceiling cracks instead. I didn't want to look around because I didn't want to let myself admit I shared circumstance with the people I used to hand pocket change. For all the benevolent newsroom talk about rights of the impoverished, all the grandstanding I listened to or wrote in columns or nodded with during some coworker's lunchtime rant about equality—it was the plasma bank waiting room where reality matched philosophy. Here, I was just another person trying to eat.

My number was called and I got trembly when I saw the needle, which may as well have been an oilrig, complete with a derrick and a support crew of fourteen stout men. I wiped out the second it touched my skin. A nurse apparently held me upright long enough to extract.

When I recovered enough to leave, a nurse handed me an envelope.

"There's five extra bucks in there," she said. "Looks like you need it. Also, don't ever come back. We can't spare staff looking after floppers."

Mary didn't ask where the grocery money came from, a great mercy on her part.

•

"It's getting cold," she said one afternoon in November as she climbed through the window after inspecting the garden. "I need a coat." Our crop had been in the ground for weeks but nothing had poked through the dirt. We took turns checking every few hours—obsessively, like the way we used to check email. I stopped typing at advertisement copy for a Greek-Thai fusion restaurant and checked my flimsy wallet. Twenty-six dollars, I counted. She watched over my shoulder. Mary didn't say a word, but I knew from the way she inhaled deep and emptied her lungs slowly that she hadn't meant a tattered one, somebody's leftovers. Second-hand clothes had been okay, when they were ironic.

"As soon as I finish up," I told her. "I have to find a signal and send this anyway."

In the back of the Salvation Army store, a rail thin employee wrestled to maneuver a vacuum cleaner. At the counter, a young man with a scraggly beard fiddled with his cell phone.

"Ten minutes to closing, folks," he said as the door shut behind us. "Make it quick."

Mary walked to the coat rack and flipped through the smalls. I remembered how she looked the first time I saw her, the way her sundress flowed so perfectly with each step, the way it draped the edges of her shoulders. I turned away as she picked through those coats, their once-black wool faded grey, their cotton worn threadbare, their imitation leather stained and torn. I didn't want to imagine her in those awful, shapeless things. I didn't want to admit that was the best we could do. I stared at nasty brown water spots on the drop ceiling, at a rack of worn-out harlequin romances and National Geographic magazines that covered the back wall. I tried to ignore her while she shopped, but I couldn't shut out the sound of those damned hangers screeching against the rack. I told myself we weren't alone in this. We had a roof and our rent was just a few months south of current. We were doing better than most in our neighborhood. We were young and smart. A year earlier, *we'd* been the ones dropping off coats. If I'd known then how it really felt to *need* one of them, I doubt I could've brought myself to donate.

The sound of hangers stopped and I imagined she'd found something. I turned, in case she was holding it for my approval or trying it on in the mirror, but all I saw was the top of Mary's head as she leaned forward, her head in her arms against the rack.

I heard her sob. I stepped forward and held her. She stood up but kept her face down, buried against my shoulder.

"Closing up," the bearded man said. He sounded perturbed. He was tossing a tennis ball in the air, chomping a massive wad of gum. I've never hit anyone in my life, but if I could've brought myself to let Mary go in that instant, he'd have been the first. I held her tighter and cradled my hand around the back of her head. Then, she stood, wiped both eyes and said, "Come on," in a tone even and cool as I'd ever heard her. She led me out of the store, calmly with even strides like nothing had happened. She even thanked the clerk with hardly a hint of bite while I followed her into the cold. She held my hand tight on the way home.

My thoughts turned melodramatic during that walk; I ran through all the bills and wondered which ones we might've neglected. If something could go wrong, that day seemed ripe for a pile-on. I imagined a past-due notice taped over our key slot, or a discovery that the phone lacked a dial tone—thus explaining why Mary hadn't gotten any calls about work. But when we arrived, the locks were unimpeded, and the dial tone rang clear. The water ran, and even though we couldn't afford it, I turned up the heat two degrees and hoped it would somehow make Mary feel better. I sat down to re-write my resume for the hundredth time, and when I went to the kitchen for water, I noticed Mary had turned the thermostat back down. I stuck my head in the bedroom, and she had on a second sweatshirt—it puffed her to twice her normal size.

"Love you," she said when she looked up.

"I love you too," I blurted—too fast, too eager to keep myself from wondering how long it'd been since we'd said those words.

The next morning, I ran downstairs to grab someone else's *Plain Dealer* subscription from the stoop. I figured it couldn't hurt to peek, so long as it was back in its wrapper before its actual owner woke.

No writing gigs, but there was a call for laborers—a developer was demolishing a steel mill and they needed help clearing rubble after the wrecking ball had its way. They mentioned no requisite experience, just one stipulation: "Work gloves a must." Once the sort of thing I presented editors as story fodder, this was now work. I wrote the address on my wrist and jogged upstairs to dress.

Sitting up against the headboard with her arms folded across a pillow, Mary pressed until I finally told her where I was going. She paused, like she was trying to figure the end of a joke that hadn't quite registered, then she laughed and laughed. I could tell she was trying to stop, didn't want to hurt my feelings, but she couldn't quit.

"You won't last five minutes," she said. "Come back to bed."

"It's worth a try." At that point, she quit laughing and looked a little scared.

"I'll be careful. Promise."

I took a bus the wrong way, out toward the suburbs, then trudged across three intersections to a hardware store. The cheapest pair of gloves was eleven dollars—approximately three meals' worth of Mary's meticulous budget. I waved down the first worker I could find—a grizzled old man with steel colored eyebrows that touched each other in the center of his forehead—and asked for something cheaper.

He looked at me, right into my eyes and I wondered whether he thought I was crazy for needing work gloves or crazy for not being able to afford even the flimsy ones I held up.

He spoke in the quiet voice of someone who hadn't yet consumed enough coffee. "What do you need them for, son?"

"A job downtown," I said. "Demolition."

"You don't look like a laborer," he said. "Sure you want to do that? It's rough. Real rough."

"Writer, laborer, crook—whatever it takes to keep my wife warm. I'd rather it not be the last one."

The old man nodded. He looked around, scratched his stubbly chin. "Meet me by the loading bay."

I walked through the automatic doors and circled to the lumberyard. He lifted up a bay door and stepped outside.

"I shouldn't do this." He looked up to see where the security cameras were located, then shifted his body. "But I'm thinking you need 'em more than me."

He took his company gloves from his apron and handed them over.

I took them. My instinct was to say, *are you sure*, or *I can't*. But all that came out was, "Thanks."

"Go take care of your sweetheart."

I took a couple steps and turned to wave, but the door was already down.

•

A line of men waited at the gate—big, burly ones. Some pointed and chuckled when I joined the line, but most didn't care who the hell was there. They held cups of gas station coffee, steel lunch pails, six-packs of energy drinks. The foreman studied me and raised his eyebrows. I waited for the laughter, but he just said, "Gloves?"

I pulled the cotton freebies from my pocket.

"Congratulations," he said. Mary would've loved his tone. "You're hired. Sign here, here, and here. We pay cash at quitting time. Don't get yourself killed, and if you got no insurance, don't let anybody know." He pointed toward a crew. I walked fast— partially to keep from thinking too hard about what I'd done, partially to keep warm. The crew chief shook my hand hard, like he was trying to break it to spare himself the trouble of issuing instructions. I survived, so he pointed and directed. I spent the next ten hours lifting hunks of a place where people used to make a decent living—clearing a dead mill so someone could build a high-end mall. I wondered which unaffordable store would occupy the ground where I stood, or whose Mercedes might park there. Before long, work killed the impulse to think. I just moved, breathed—mechanical.

Mary found a thermos that night at the dollar store. For the rest of the week, she got up and heated off-brand soup in the microwave, filled the big red jug for me and sealed it tight, sent me out the door with a kiss, then went back to listen for her phone.

The Berlin Pillow Wall crumbled slowly, and our bodies rested slightly closer each night that week. When our hands touched in bed I felt her fingertips trace my newly calloused palms. I anticipated, those first days, new curves on my biceps and triceps, and steel-plated abs to replace my own natural arc. But I stayed slight, the only tangible evidence of my labor was ripped up hands and finger joints that ached when I sat under lamplight in the evenings and typed.

The last day of the gig, when the junk was cleared and the grading equipment was lined up and spitting diesel, our foreman patted my back, told me I was tough for a stringy thing. Said I'd be welcome on any other jobs.

"Any coming up?"

He spat and shook his head. "Keep watching the papers. We're all job-to-job like you."

•

I set aside the next month's bills and took the leftover fifty dollars to an outlet. After an hour scouring the racks, I found a black wool pea coat, discounted because the liner was torn. But I could fix it, put everything back together—just a needle and some thread, no one would ever see the scar. I got a scarf, too, and cheap black mittens. I folded all that fabric into a bundle and hid it behind my back when I walked into the apartment. But she wasn't there. I looked out the window first, to see if she was brushing snow off the garden. Nothing. I checked her room for a note. Nothing. I thought maybe she got a sub call, and grinned ear-to-ear over it. I imagined ongoing assignments for her and steady paychecks, and—better yet—dinner stories about how her students were learning and how she was making a difference. I thought that if it had finally worked out for her, maybe there was hope for me—maybe one of the guys who always sent me his work overflow would find a better job elsewhere. Maybe in Portland. I was so hopeful, I opened the window and got ready to step out on the fire escape, certain that I'd find a blossom or bloom or sprout outside, certain it was finally *our* day, that we'd turned the corner—then it hit me she could be gone altogether.

That I'd been too slow and too poor and too frail the whole time, that she'd finally given up.

I slumped onto the curled-up linoleum and felt something far worse than what poverty had created: the excruciating quiet of alone. My face was in my hands when the deadbolt clicked, and Mary walked in wearing a faded gray coat from the thrift shop, its elbows threadbare and its collar shapeless.

"What's that?" I asked. My voice was edgy, I know. It had to have been.

She worked to produce a smile. "I found a coat," she said. She whirled around to show me, and as she was spinning she saw the shopping bag on top of the table.

"Is that—"

I nodded." She shrugged out of her coat and hugged me the way a mother hugs a kid who just lost a fight.

"I'll take it back for you," she said. "That was sweet of you. But we can't—"

"Please keep it."

She opened the bag, put on the scarf first, then the mittens, then the coat.

"You're so beautiful," I told her, and she walked to the bathroom mirror to look herself over. She even flipped back her hair, moved her head around to see herself in different lights. "This is what I thought of every day at the mill. It's torn inside but I'll match the thread and—"

"Thank you," she said again. She looked at the price tags as she carefully removed and folded each item. She cringed when she saw the coat price. The worst part was that such a small number had become luxury.

"Tell you what—I'll keep the scarf and mittens, and I'll keep my coat. The money from your coat, we'll save for the next thing that goes wrong. Eventually, we'll have more money than things going wrong and you can buy me any coat you want."

I didn't want to nod, but my head moved anyway.

In the morning, she put on her grey coat to brace against the wind as she took the new one away, its lining still torn, the receipt folded in her pocket. As she blew a kiss in the doorway, the beaten-up fabric served as an agent of contrast that somehow made her look even lovelier. So far removed from that wispy sundress girl, she looked determined and strong. I wondered how differently I must look to her—or whether she'd even noticed a change. I watched from the window as she walked away. She flipped her collar up against the wind, but it flopped back to her shoulders.

•

Spinach was the first thing we harvested from the garden. I hate spinach, but that one day, I loved it, savored its taste and texture. I loved the meal even more when two days passed and no one needed an ambulance. Mary wears her coat when she takes a bus to the suburbs to walk dogs for people who answer her Craigslist ads, and she wore it last Monday when Garfield Middle School needed a fill-in classroom aide. She's been called back twice, and each time the phone rings I get out of bed with her and walk downstairs to check the paper.

She probably thinks about Portland when she's in the classroom—reconnects with that old feeling of immeasurable possibility. That makes me even more ashamed of our tenement and its ill-fitting windows, which is probably more run-down even than her squatter's warehouse. But I love her tiny repairs, even if she doesn't think I notice: liquid paper over the paint cracks near our headboard, last-leg flowers salvaged from a café, my framed sad article obscuring some prior resident's wall-punch. When she comes home from work, she smiles, and I kiss her at the door—I kiss her because I've missed her and because she hasn't fled and because of those beautiful, hopeful, inexplicable plants that keep emerging from the loamy clay outside.

I brought today's paper upstairs because of the call for workers to tear out a building's innards for a condo conversion.

I went to retrieve a pen, and by the time I found one Mary was hunched over the front page, reading the headline article. "Jesus," she said, and she looked pale. "Jesus." She held it up to show me the headline before she checked her watch and sat for a calm sip or two of coffee before heading off to work.

I felt no joy when I read that article about how the Youngstown paper folded altogether. I wondered, by instinct, which upstart corporation would take over the building. I wondered, too, about the workers who made it to the end—what their resumes look like, whether they'd come to the city and jump into the freelancing pool, or whether they'd elbow their way ahead of me in day labor lines or shrug and move back in with their parents, or whether they'd disappear to Portland until they figured out what to make of themselves. Mary got up from the table and gathered her things for work. As she left one more time and I sat behind once more to wait, I figured they'd all turn out about the same in the end, regardless.

moving day

No matter where Sadie Hayes went to school, she was always top of her class in geography. It was spelling that she had trouble with: just about the time she figured out how to arrange the letters of each new town, her mother would pick her up at school, the suitcases already packed and stacked in the back seat. Sadie's mom said the same thing every time, the same two words and little else: "Sorry, kid."

Sadie had already figured out how to spell Topeka and Atlanta, Mobile and Nashville.

Sorry, kid.

She never bothered with Ashtabula—Cleveland was just down the street, and much easier to spell. Baton Rouge had been hard (it wasn't spelled at all the way it sounded) but she was in Pittsburgh just long enough that she remembered to give it both *T*'s and an *H*.

Sorry, kid.

Frankfort and Springfield and Evansville were easy enough, but now Sadie was irritated to be learning Huntington, reminding herself again and again to remember that first *T*.

Sorry, kid.

She liked her new school, a large old brick square with crumbly stairs and three tall chimneys rising up out of the roof. On the bus, she made quick friends with Danielle, a girl who wore her black hair in pigtails, whose pink plastic shoes sparkled, and whose dresses always seemed to be new. After a week in Huntington, Sadie's mother suggested she do what she'd done so often before with so many new friends: she invited Danielle to sleep over, to visit her home. To keep her company. The girls exchanged telephone numbers, and that evening when the phone rang Sadie listened through her bedroom wall as her mother worked out the details of the sleepover. She resisted the urge to smile until she heard the magic words: "Friday at six, then. Perfect."

Friday after school, Sadie's mother helped her assemble a pup tent in the fenced-in backyard. Sadie was waiting on the doorstep when Danielle and her mother arrived in a shiny silver car that had no top. Danielle stayed in that car for what seemed like ages—her mother reached and turned up the car stereo so loud that Sadie could hear the song's thump-thump-thump rhythm, then leaned over to whisper something into her daughter's ear. Danielle's head bobbed and shook, bobbed and shook at whatever things her mother said. This went on for a few moments until Sadie's mother came out onto the front porch, arms outstretched in a yawn. She was wearing a pair of torn jean shorts and a white tube top, no shoes. Sadie understood this would probably not help things, and the longer her new friend remained in the parked car, the more Sadie wondered if Danielle's mother might drive away without even letting Danielle out of the car. But Danielle's mother finally made a sad face and handed over a cell phone, waved a small little wave toward Sadie and her mother.

As soon as Danielle shut the car door, her mom backed out of the driveway and tore off. The tires squealed as she changed directions and went away. Sadie liked that sound of hurry, but it was the arrival of a new friend that made Sadie happiest, and so she ran off the porch to hug Danielle.

"Hi, Kiddo," Sadie's mom said. The words sounded extra long and a little slow. "Lemme show you where the toilet's at, then you can take your stuff out to the tent."

•

Danielle deposited her purple sleeping roll and matching overnight bag on the stained tent floor, and then Sadie showed Danielle the best game she could think of in this new backyard: bouncing a rubber ball against the cinder block wall of the house. Each girl managed just a few bounces before the back window slid open and Sadie's mom shouted, "Knock it off!" The window slammed and Sadie dropped the ball. She looked around the yard, trying to think of something else to do. Tag would work if there were more kids, and there was always storytelling, but that was more of an after-dark thing.

"There's sure not much to look at back here," Danielle finally said.

She was right, Sadie knew. The grass was all beaten down, with brown patches of dirt peeking through. A smelly doghouse and rusted chain sat in the corner, left behind by a previous renter. The fence was tall and wooden with no cracks, which prevented the girls from peeking past to see what was happening out in the world. But there *was* a gate.

"Wait here," Sadie said. "I have an idea."

•

Sadie knocked on her mother's bedroom door. As she waited for an answer, she saw through the front picture window's thin curtain that a strange car was parked in the gravel driveway. The doors were three different colors, with spots of rust blossoming on the hood. There was always a car whenever Sadie was allowed to sleep in the tent. Sometimes they were nice and shiny, but mostly they looked like this one. Still, Sadie smiled, glad her mom made new friends quickly, too.

"What?" her mother's voice called from the inside. "What'd you two do?"

"Nothing, Momma. I just want to know if we can *move*."

"What are you talking about, child?"

Sadie heard rustling inside the room.

"There's nothing to do here," Sadie said. "Can we move?"

"Fine, fine, whatever," her mom said. "Sure. We'll—we'll talk about it later, okay? You need to get back outside with your friend."

"Okay," Sadie said, trying not to sound too excited. Every time she sounded too excited about something, her mom changed her mind.

Sadie grinned, though, at her mother's permission and skipped out the back door.

"Let's pull up the stakes," Sadie said. "We're moving."

"Moving?"

"Yeah. Just like Mom and me do. Let's find a better place to camp."

And then Sadie added something her mother often told her on the way to some new, unknown place: "It's for the best."

"You're crazy."

"No," Sadie said. "I promise, it'll be fun."

Danielle reached into her pocket and pulled out her mom's phone. She tapped it with her thumb and it lit up.

"Don't," Sadie said. "Don't leave. It'll be an adventure. A real adventure—our first one together. Don't you want an adventure?"

"Not really," Danielle said. "We have three hundred channels at home."

"Can I come with you then?"

"Probably not."

"So, you're just going to leave me?"

Danielle sighed and looked around. "I guess I can't leave you *here* on your own."

"So, we'll move then?"

"If you say so," Danielle said. "It's your sleepover."

Danielle put on her backpack and Sadie ran inside to grab her own. She filled it with a clean pair of shorts and a shirt and she scooped up a handful of the candy she'd stashed away in her sock drawer. They would need food along the way, she was sure. Outside, she pulled up the tent stakes and put them into the bag, along with the hammer she and her mother used to assemble the tent.

They rolled their sleeping bags and made for the gate, each with a sleeping bag in one hand and an edge of tent in the other. They both had to shove, but the heavy, rusted hinge eventually gave way. They stretched the tent to make it fit and walked through, leaving the gate wide open in case they needed to get back inside.

The girls found themselves in an alley between other gates, a row of identical backyards with laundry lines hanging overhead.

"Which way?" Sadie asked.

"Hmm." Danielle hesitated and looked both directions. Sadie wondered which one she would pick, even though there didn't seem to be much difference in the choices. Danielle finally shrugged and said, "Left. Let's go left."

And so they went left, through the midsection of the Washington Park Federal Housing Project. When the alley emptied out onto West Twenty-Second Street, they waited until the crosswalk sign turned white, and they marched across four lanes of traffic. They passed plenty of people on the sidewalk, people who looked down at the concrete or whose eyes darted around. No one seemed to notice the girls, or else they looked away fast, like they were doing it on purpose. Sadie felt invisible, but this time, it felt nice. It felt free. She led Danielle and the tent past all those people, past shops with rusty iron bars on the doors and buildings with boards covering the windows. They watched a man bend over and throw up on the ground, and then laughed, just as they'd done when Jimmie Martin puked on the school bus and the driver had to pull over and cover it up with pink stuff that looked like cat litter.

•

On a sidewalk that ran along Division Street, a man finally noticed the girls, and he walked right up to them. Sadie waved.

"Where are you two beautiful young ladies taking that tent off to?" The man's jeans had holes in their knees, his lips were dry and scabbed. He was missing a tooth, maybe even two—right up in the front of his mouth. Stringy gray hair fell over his forehead. He smiled a strange smile.

"We're moving," Sadie told him.

"Looking for a new campground," Danielle added. "The old one was bo-ring."

"Well, that so?" the man asked. He smiled wider and set his hand on the fabric of the tent. He brushed his pointer finger over the fabric, as if he'd never felt anything like it before. That finger wagged back and forth for a minute until he spoke again: "I've got a place you can bring it."

"Really?" Sadie asked.

"It's a pretty place," he said. "Here, come along real quick and I'll show it to you."

"I don't know," Danielle said. "Mom told me not to—"

Sadie felt a hand on her shoulder—a big, firm hand—and whipped around. A fat woman with a round, shiny face and curly hair had hold of her, but the lady wasn't looking at Sadie at all. She was staring hard and mean at the man with the missing tooth. "You leave these girls alone," she said, her voice loud enough that people on the sidewalk and even on the other side of the road turned to look. "You can pester the ones your own age, you hear?"

Sadie turned back to the man, who was no longer smiling. He opened up his mouth to speak, but said nothing, and then turned and shuffled off. He looked back over his shoulder as he walked, watching the woman, not the girls.

"Didn't your mothers ever tell you not to talk to strangers?" the lady asked.

Danielle slumped her shoulders and said, "Yes, ma'am," but Sadie couldn't say anything. Her mother had never told her that. And every few months, *everyone* was a stranger all over again. It would have sounded silly if her Mom *had* said it.

"You two get on home now," the woman said. "This ain't no campground, and it ain't no place for little girls, either."

"Yes, ma'am," Danielle said again, and the two of them started walking—further away from Sadie's home.

When they turned the corner and were alone, they laughed and laughed. They laughed about the man's teeth and laughed at the way the woman's belly fell way down past the bottom of her shirt. Sadie laughed because she knew no other way to react. Her body told her she should respond somehow—her heart pounded, she started to sweat, her fingers tingled. She *had* to laugh. And because Danielle laughed, too, Sadie supposed that she was right to laugh. So they kept laughing right up until the dog had its teeth on the back of Danielle's shiny plastic shoe. Sadie didn't see him from her side of the tent and so she kept walking until she felt the tent tug loose from her hand and turned to see Danielle, no longer walking, standing pale with her mouth and eyes opened wide.

"What is it?" Sadie asked.

"Dog!" Danielle hissed. "Big, big dog!"

The hair stood up on the back of Sadie's neck. She walked on tiptoes around the tent's edge until she saw the dog, a gray, growling thing with lots of mean in its eyes. Its nose was against Danielle's ankle, one of its teeth caught on the strappy back of her jelly shoe. Without thinking and in one swift motion, Sadie took the backpack off her shoulders and whipped it at the angry-looking dog's head. The tent spikes and hammer jingled as they made contact with the dog, which jerked its head backward and yanked Danielle's shoe off her foot. Danielle fell forward as her foot was pulled out from under her, and the dog raced down the street, a shiny shoe hanging from its mouth.

Sadie helped Danielle up. "Are you okay?" she asked.

Danielle's knee was scraped and bloody, but she didn't even have a tear in her eye. She stood there for a second without doing anything and then, all of a sudden, her mouth shaped itself into the hugest smile Sadie had ever seen. Danielle stepped forward and hugged her.

"You saved me from the evil dog-beast!" Danielle said. "You're my hero!"

Sadie didn't feel like a hero. Instead, she worried—was the dog okay? She didn't like the idea of hitting things, even when they'd been mean to her. But she was happy that her friend was safe. That was what mattered the most. Danielle was safe and relieved and smiling.

"Where should we go next?" Sadie asked.

Danielle looked around.

"I don't know much about this part of the city," she said. "Mom drives so fast anytime we're here."

"Well, we'd better find a place to camp," Sadie said, and Danielle nodded. They picked up their tent and kept going.

Block after block, they hiked, stopping and starting with the crosswalk lights, some of which never changed at all. Others had flashing blue lights at the top.

Just after they crossed the intersection of Division and Third Avenue, Sadie looked up and noticed that it was getting dark, that the sky had lost almost all its blue, that half the streetlights were already on, and the rest were flashing and flickering, trying hard to work. The tent was getting heavy, and without sunlight they wouldn't be able to put it up anyway. Sadie exhaled and felt helpless: you can't put a tent stake into the sidewalk.

"There," Danielle said, and pointed.

"Perfect," Sadie said, and they walked fast.

•

Between the girls and the hill was a stretch of train tracks—twelve of them lined up side-to-side, all leading toward a sooty, tall old building with giant black piles at its edge and smoke pouring out of four great chimneys, the likes of which she'd never seen in all those strangely spelled towns, from Mobile to Ashtabula.

One last challenge, Sadie thought as she looked over the tracks. They were almost there.

As they reached the first track, Danielle slowed down, and then stopped altogether.

"I don't think we should," she said. "Mom told me trains are *dangerous*."

"These aren't trains, silly, just train *tracks*," Sadie said. "We have to be careful, but we can do it."

"The rocks will hurt my foot. And I'm tired already. Let's go back." Danielle folded her arms across her chest and pooched out her bottom lip. Sadie knew this face—it was one she'd used on her own mother, the look she saved for when nothing else had worked. She reached out and pushed Danielle's pouty lip back into place, which made her smile, even though she kept her arms folded. But as soon as Sadie removed her hand, Danielle stopped smiling and repeated, "I'm tired. Let's go home."

Sadie hadn't thought of it, but she was tired, too. They'd moved a long way. She wondered if they were still in Huntington with two *T*s, or if they'd walked so far they were in some brand new place with a new name. She thought about her mother back at home—hoped she was having as much fun with her friend as Sadie was with Danielle. But her mother was far away now and so was home—unreachable. Sadie looked forward and saw how close they were to that perfect camping spot, green and beautiful and so calm compared to all the places they'd walked. They couldn't stop now, not this close to the perfect sleeping spot. Sadie looked at the track, then up at her friend who was planted in place. Sadie set down her side of the tent and walked around it until she was facing Danielle. There were tears in her friend's eyes. Sadie wiped her hand on her shorts before reaching up and gently flicking each tear away, the way her own mother had in the middle of so many unwanted moves.

"Mom will come get us," Danielle said, begging. "I can call her. Please…"

"No," Sadie said. She thought that if Danielle's mom came, they would go home, to separate houses. The sleepover would be finished. "Here, wear these. I like to walk barefoot anyway."

"Really?"

"Friends are supposed to share, right?"

"I guess so."

Danielle put the shoes on, and the girls picked up their tent, ready for the final yards of their trip.

"Remember to look both ways before each track," Sadie said.

"I know, silly."

Together, they hobbled their way across the tracks, counted them out loud until they'd passed the last one, number twelve. They walked down into a dry ditch with concrete walls and then climbed back up the other side. With each step, a different sharp or hard or rough surface—pushed into the bottoms of Sadie's feet. She felt a new pain with each stride. She squeezed her hands into fists and bit her bottom lip. But Sadie did not complain. Sadie climbed the first half of a tall grass-covered wall and then stopped to wait while Danielle caught her breath. When they reached the top, they stared out over the edge. Sadie's heart beat hard again, part from the climb and part from the view. On one side, a barge slid slowly down the still, wide river. On the other, the city lights danced and flickered.

"It's perfect," Danielle said. "Beautiful."

"The best move I've ever had," Sadie said. "We should stay here forever."

They set the tent down on the grass. Sadie took the stakes and the hammer out of her bag and fastened the tent to the ground. She tried to show Danielle how to do it, the way her own mother had taught her. But Danielle was more interested in the boats and the lights and the tiny stars that were just starting to show up at the very top of the sky. So Sadie fastened the tent herself. They crawled inside, placed their sleeping bags next to each other, and lay down. Sadie wrapped an arm around her new friend and snuggled up next to her, just like her mother had done in so many tents and motel rooms and new homes.

"Goodnight, Kiddo," she said to Danielle, but her friend was already asleep.

•

The man who woke Sadie held a flashlight and kept saying, "Little girl, are you okay? Little girl, are you okay?"

Sadie sat up and said, "Shhh! My friend is sleeping." But then she looked around the tent and saw that Danielle wasn't there. "Where did she go? Where is Danielle?"

"It's okay," the man said. "She's outside. I'm officer Brady. You can't camp here, okay? It's not safe. We're going to take you someplace that is."

"Why can't we stay?" she asked. "It is too safe."

"This isn't your home," he said. "Come on outside."

Outside the tent, another officer was talking on Danielle's cell phone. Sadie heard the loud, angry voice on the other end of the phone and figured there would probably not be any more sleepovers with her new friend. Danielle smiled, though, and Sadie could tell she was trying hard not to laugh. The officer kept saying, "Ma'am, please calm down. Please calm down." Every time he said this, Danielle's mom yelled even louder.

"Why did you two girls run away?" Officer Brady asked Sadie.

"We're not running away, silly," she said. "We just moved. Mom moves all the time."

•

At the station, officers gave Sadie and Danielle dolls to play with, but they just sat and kicked their legs in chairs too high for their feet to reach the ground.

"Can we have our tent back?" Danielle asked.

"Sorry, honey," a policewoman said. "That's evidence."

"What's evidence for?" Sadie asked.

"Don't you worry about that," the woman said, and patted Sadie's head. Sadie didn't like when people patted her head. It's what people always did when something was happening that wasn't supposed to happen. It was usually about her mom.

•

Danielle's mother had already picked her up (and given Sadie an angry look) by the time Sadie's mother burst in the door, picked her up and swung her around in a big hug, then set her down and kneeled so that they were looking straight into each other's eyes.

"No more moving, okay, kid?" Sadie's mom said.

"Promise?"

"No, honey, I meant—" Sadie's mother stopped, froze up like she couldn't figure out how to finish.

Sorry, kid.

She just stood there, her mouth wide-open staring back at Sadie until Officer Brady placed his hand on her left shoulder, said, "Ma'am, we'll need to ask you a few questions." She nodded slowly at the man and then blew her daughter a kiss.

Sorry, kid.

Sadie watched her mom follow officer Brady and a policewoman down a long hallway and then through a door that slammed hard once they were all through. Sadie found one of the stained, green chairs in the lobby and sat down to wait for whichever grownup would arrive to try and cheer her up.

Sorry, kid.

On the table rested a pile of magazines, but Sadie did not reach for one, not even the one about geography. In her green chair, she wondered which new place they would explore next, which new spelling she would learn, which new friends she and her mother might make. She sat and she spelled and she waited and she waited and she waited for the door to open.

destroying new boston

There was no reason for us to believe there would be diesel in the tank. We'd watched that mill decay since childhood, while unemployed and under-employed fathers threw back six-packs and cursed its existence. Why would the crane have still had juice?

It was comical to watch Edith scamper up the substructure of the crane and do her goofy little dance at the top. But, being Edith, she had to take things a step farther, and that's when it all went down. She hopped into the cab and set right to jabbing buttons, pulling levers, kicking at the foot pedals. She sat down in the operator's stool and waved. That's when Jake noticed it.

"Did you guys hear something?"

We did—the rumble of an engine, followed shortly by a god-awful guttural groaning. The sound of gears turning.

I flailed my arms in warning, but between the height, the angles, and what I imagine must've been a special blend of terror, she couldn't see a thing. Sam and Jake screamed at me to stop but I didn't pay them any mind and I launched myself up the ladder, leapt into the cab where Edith was frozen in place, her eyes open wide and her skin somehow paler than normal—even her freckles seemed to have gone pure white. That's when I did what any teenaged would-be hero must: I slammed every button I could find, including the big red joystick in the middle. In hindsight, that's one I should've avoided. But somewhere in the frenzy of my motion, I whacked it. Jarred it to the right, where it stuck. The hulking machine turned clockwise. It moved real slow at first, but by the end of the first revolution it was already spinning at a good clip.

Edith unfroze long enough to turn toward me and shout over the motor's racket: "Jump?"

We grabbed each other's hand and did just that. We cleared the cab, tumbled onto the platform, and then hurried down a rusty ladder to the ground. The cab spun in faster circles. The crane arm, its cable, and the attached hook became a giant whip—a wrecking ball. It hit a small coal shed first—that ramshackle job of rebar and corrugated steel sheets stood no chance. The hook broadsided the main coke oven and must've struck dead on a main beam, because that building, the most recognizable piece of our miserable little city, trembled for about ten seconds, and then collapsed on itself. I followed my friends toward the street, not yet feeling the cuts, scrapes and bruises I'd gathered in my fall. Behind our backs, we heard a crash—a small section of the mill's conveyor lines crashing into the Ohio River.

When we reached the abandoned Norfolk-Southern yard, we turned around and stared at the aftermath, breathless, terrified, accidentally triumphant. Jake wore the biggest grin I'd ever seen on him, and Sam just stared blankly. Though I never saw him with a joint, I to this day suspect that Sam was either perpetually stoned or deeply frayed, emotionally. In that moment, though, he was blank with *awe*. Edith and I looked at each other, wide-eyed for a moment. Then, we surveyed our handiwork and waited for our hearts to return to normal tempo.

"Dude," Jake said. "You two just destroyed New Boston."

Of course, we hadn't—we'd just destroyed the part of New Boston that had destroyed the rest of New Boston. The plant that put all our fathers and most of our mothers out of work. But that was good enough to count for destroying the place, wasn't it? Much better than our normal Tuesday routine, which involved splitting a six-pack of generic soda and chucking rocks from the bluff-top high school parking lot.

We would later swear that we presided over our triumph until the first of the plant's stacks tipped over and came hurtling directly at us. In reality, it was the sound of approaching sirens that prompted retreat. Running, I thought of my father's face the night the plant closed, how he'd come home and sat down as if nothing had happened. His eyes were so blank and empty that night, his face bland and expressionless. He shut the blinds, then slumped all night on the sofa and stared at the black television screen —he never used to shut those blinds, so I knew right away that something was wrong. Bad wrong. Later that night when I snuck out of bed and peeked through them, I saw, for the first time, what the nighttime skyline looked like without a pilot light blazing. Dad never looked the same to me after that night. The color never fully returned to his face, the life never completely returned to his eyes. So as I hurdled pieces of wreckage, I smiled for him. I smiled for all the fathers and families whose trajectories were flattened by this place. I imagined that if Dad had known the plant could be so easily destroyed, he'd have chugged a longneck or five and climbed into that crane years earlier.

•

We thought it was over—we didn't expect the aftershock. It must've been the sudden resumption of motion at the long-dormant site, all that stored up energy hidden in an epoch's worth of packed soot and we'd set it loose. We reached the top of the hill, our normal roost, just in time to see the first brick smokestack fall, right across the rail lines where we'd stood ten minutes earlier. Edith's eyes got all wide, and Sam gave Jake a look that was full of nothing but panic.

A few seconds later, as if waiting for the cue of our full attention, the easternmost stack crumbled. The center stack, the tallest one, wavered for a few seconds, like a great middle finger, flipping one last bird at the town before it collapsed on itself— straight down in a pile like its spine had suddenly become jelly.

"Dude," Sam said, his tone even-keeled and bored as ever. "That's not real good."

Jake faced Edith, grabbed her by the belt, pulled her against him, wrapped his arm around her back and kissed her. After a few seconds of frantic slurping, Jake let her go, staggered backward. "You are a god," he said.

"Yep," she replied. We all watched her. It seemed as though she desperately wanted to say something else, something important. Maybe something that would change *everything*.

Whatever it was, it never got traction. She just smiled and repeated, "Yep."

•

A couple hours later, we were screwing around inside the Dollar General, avoiding our homes—we looked fine to each other but knew our parents would take one look at us and know it was absolutely our fault.

"They're looking for you, you know." The clerk—I couldn't remember her name since she'd quit coming to school earlier in the year and hadn't really done anything notable while there—said this very matter-of-factly.

"For what?" Jake asked.

The clerk just laughed at him.

He stepped forward and placed his hands on the counter as if he was going to intimidate her. "How the hell do they even know? And who is *they*?"

She pointed at the store's police scanner, turned on low behind the counter.

"Somebody saw you running, told the cops," the girl said, then she smiled. "Take some gum on your way out. On me."

I grabbed a pack of Winterfresh, but put it back when no one else took any.

Around the corner at Wippy Dip, the manager leaned through the service window and gave us a thumbs-up.

"How the hell do these people even know who we are?" I whispered to Edith. "And who told?"

"I don't know," she said. "Maybe it'd help if you didn't look so guilty. Stop looking guilty." I guess she could tell it was striking me right then that we were about to be in it deep over what we'd done, so she playfully smacked my shoulder to take the edge off her remark. It didn't work.

Meanwhile, Jake was stalking up to the window like he does when he's pissed. He looked like he was about to deck the poor burger guy, and so we all stopped to see what would happen.

Jake leaned forward, and what we wouldn't have given to hear what he said then, but when he turned around a minute later, he had an armful of burgers and fries. "Our reward," he said, and we took over a picnic table.

"What about drinks?" Sam asked.

"Shut up and eat your fries," Jake said.

I didn't understand how they could be so calm to just sit and eat like that, out in public, in the middle of everything. We were fugitives—people with badges were out there searching for us, and someone had already taken the liberty of ratting us out. I managed about five bites of food; while they joked around and told stories about gym class, I focused most of my energy on repressing vomit.

·

When the last burger wrapper was pitched into a steel trashcan—the kind that gets chained up to a post in places like this—Jake told us to follow him, which kind of went without saying. We followed him most of the time as it was, but the rest of us were particularly okay with following in this instance since he was the only one with real experience running from anything. He'd been in juvie at least three times, so when it came to the wrong side of the law, the rest of us were spotless enough to defer to him. Even went into places we had no desire to go, but we hung back for a moment when he strolled through the windowless door of the Brass Pony Club—just strutted right in like he'd been there a hundred times. A second later, he stuck his head out the door and waved us in.

"Time to celebrate," Jake said. The rest of us looked at each other and shrugged. Edith was the first one who finally stepped forward. If she was okay with it, there wasn't any good excuse left to stay outside.

None of us were eighteen and we were all dead broke. It took about five minutes for us to realize that a strip club was a really dumb place to be with empty pockets and a preexisting guilt complex, so we filed right back out. Still, we'd been inside, and we were pretty certain that would carry some nice lunchroom cred. On the way out, a manager with a lopsided goatee shook our hands, congratulated us and said, "Make sure y'all come see us again when you get out." He kept up at cackling until the door clanked shut. We had won over the town's elite, clearly.

Sam insisted on walking once around the block, since he figured some of the girls might be out back smoking and that they might be interested in giving out some kind of hero reward, but all we found was an empty picnic table that lilted a bit toward the building. The rest of the space was empty save for about ten thousand cigarette butts, each one stained with a different tone of lipstick.

Once we cleared the block, Jake pointed toward the river. "Bridge?" he asked.

"Bridge," Sam confirmed, and we made for the riverfront, scaled the overland tresswork of the L&N Railroad Bridge. Despite red-lettered *Beware* signs posted everywhere, it was perfectly safe to climb. The coal trains coming up from Kentucky had gotten so long and so heavy they had to cross the new, gleaming, reinforced bridge east of Huntington—New Boston wasn't even viable as a shortcut.

Jake reached back to help Edith up, but she climbed onto the deck herself, scrambling with a hilarious leg kick. Even though the deck's steel grate was woven tight enough for someone to walk on, we balanced on the rails, stopped midway and sat, dangled legs out over the river. We gazed back at town, at the new skyline we'd created.

"Looks even more dead," Sam said.

"Just looks honest," Jake said.

The front tip of a downbound barge crept under the bridge, empty—its great open bins dingy with the last load, awaiting their next pile of coal or ore. Sam searched the deck for a suitable rock, then launched a golf ball-sized hunk of limestone at the barge. For a good ten seconds, it danced and pinged around the hopper. A crewman ran out of the pilothouse, to investigate the sound, to determine whether it was the bridge falling apart, or the barge. Sam whistled and waved at the man, who aimed his light at us and then waved back, though it was inconclusive whether he did so with his entire hand. We saw the quick flick of a lighter and then the glowing cigarette that every few seconds swung an arc between his hip and his lips, until the barge started its swing around the bend and he dropped his cig, ran into the cabin to fetch the rest of the crew. A few seconds later, his silhouette reemerged, pointing out the newly flat riverfront.

The bridge was the only point from which New Boston had ever really looked like a city, and only at night when the functionless shells of buildings stood in for all the nothingness that was *really* there. For the first time that night, we got to see our town for what we knew it to be. Behind us, to the east, twin halos of light that marked Ashland and Huntington reassured us that some places don't mind being lit, don't mind being seen as they are.

"You see that?" Edith asked.

She pointed toward the bank. Near the plant entrance, where infrastructure once stood, a couple flashlight beams bounced off of windows and guardrails.

"That's for us?" Jake asked.

I nodded.

Sam grinned a little sheepishly.

"We're freaking celebrities," Jake said.

I shook my head. "It's Tuesday. What else have they got to do?"

"Either way," Sam said, "they're going to catch us."

"Of course they are," Jake said. "But it's worth it, right?"

Nobody answered him—we all just sat there and stared at our handiwork. I looked at Sam on my right, at Jake and Edith on my left, and imagined this moment was the pinnacle for us, that we would reflect on that moment in much the same way our classmates might remember a particular football game, or being crowned homecoming queen, or having their first intentional kid. As good as it gets. I knew Sam and Jake and Edith had no plans to leave town, and even though I assumed I'd eventually move on, it seemed in that moment highly unlikely that any event in my life could ever top that night. And for the moment, that was okay—as far as seminal moments go, I could've done a lot worse. I decided it would make for the sort of story that would someday cause my kids to grimace while I told my grandkids about it in brutal, exaggerated detail. As for life pinnacles, ours was much cooler than playing a game in tight pants or spending a couple of hours in a plastic crown.

Sam chucked one last rock into the river, and we watched the resulting rings spread out and diffuse. We stood in wordless unison, balanced the rail back to shore.

•

When we turned the corner onto Sycamore, a cop car waited in Jake's driveway—his dad leaned on the cruiser, smoking and having a laugh with the men who sought his son. Jake's face turned a familiar shade of red, and I grabbed onto his wrist, pulled him backward. It wasn't going to do us any good if he socked his old man, right there in front of a cop. We made for the apartment complex where Edith's mother lived, but a city cop was smoking in the stairwell. By this point, lights were making us jumpy so we headed for Sam's through dimmer alleys. A sheriff leaned on his cruiser, which was tilted to block the driveway, as if we were going to run the blockade in our non-existent cars. My place was farthest away, and the unspoken hope was that no one had bothered to check there. They must've been out of police cars, because, honest to God, a fire truck sat waiting against the curb. Mom and Dad stood on the porch with arms folded. Mom was clearly crying. Dad had his arm wrapped around her.

Of all the people who could've spotted us, it was one of the firemen who shouted and pointed as we ducked below the fence line. We bolted, still hunched over so they wouldn't see our heads over the fence. For a moment, we tried to keep up with Jake, but he had too much experience with this sort of thing and took off into a stand of trees; we couldn't keep the pace. When he turned and paused to wait for us, Edith was the only one who made the effort to continue. Sam just shook his head and walked back toward downtown. I was a little proud of him. That was the boldest act I'd ever seen him complete. Me? I just shrugged and stayed put.

"Suit yourselves," Jake said. "Good luck."

I waited for a moment, watched them make their slow-motion getaways, toward hiding places amongst empty buildings and burnt-out streetlights. I suppose theirs was the logical choice, but I wasn't going to waste that night hiding. I went back to the mill.

•

I felt like it should be hard work getting there, and so I slipped along the brick wall of an abandoned upholstery shop, then got cute and decided to scale a fence with action-flick speed. Thank God that Dad insisted on buying us cheap jeans. I'd have been stuck hanging upside-down if they hadn't torn so easily. As it turned out, I was suspended just an instant—not even long enough to extend my arms and buffer the impact—before I plunged squarely on my head. The resulting bump, along with some mild blackening of the left eye, would look completely boss in my mug shot, I decided. It hurt less than the realization, when I stood and looked around, that absolutely no one was following me.

I used a bit more care when I hopped the limp barbed wire and re-entered the crime scene. I picked up the first blunt object that didn't seem likely to tear open my palms, scaled the nearest pile of rubble. I was done keeping quiet and holding back. When I lifted that slim vein of heavy-gauge pipe over my head ready for that first strike, I felt more powerful than I'd managed to in seventeen previous years combined. As I set my shoulder muscles into motion and sent the hollow rod screaming downward, I thought of everything else that could have possibly destroyed this place—a swollen Ohio, an explosive mishap, an earth-scorching blast at the uranium enrichment plant a few miles inland, or downstream at the nuclear power station. But *we* had done it. We had taken down the mill, and I wanted to kick it while it gasped. Just like it had done to us.

The pipe was crummy as a destructive tool, but even the smallest crack in a piece of concrete or the divorce of a few long-mortared bricks felt cathartic. When I struck, the pipe pinged and then reverberated the way my Little League bat had the day I forgot to pack batting gloves for practice. This time, I didn't complain. It was painful and clunky, but still gave more satisfaction than my truest of hits the day Dad handed me a nine iron at the driving range.

"World's best way to blow off stress," he had said, then clobbered a shot off the 150-yard sign. Until the night at the mill, I believed him.

I thought of Dad, too, as I whacked away a piece of foundation, and I knew it had to be the providence of his spirit when I found a real, honest-to-God sledgehammer, resting right out in open space, rusted, halfway sunk in a patch of mud, begging to be used again. When I made my first solid contact with that monster—God, it felt amazing. As if the world slowed as I swung so that I could feel each vein pulse and each muscle fire in a quickening chain from my legs to hips, then through my back and shoulders and arms until the hammer hit concrete and all my force and momentum stopped and my whole body shook, my fingers trembled and I saw the crumbled piece of mess I'd made out of something once solid. The sledgehammer was invented for just such a moment. I felt like the lone person who would *ever* know the instrument's proper use. I took my new implement to the highest point of the tallest rubble pile I could find and started bashing it down from the top. It was up there that I first had the sensation of not being alone. All the way on the other side of the mess we'd made, down by the barge dock, I swore I heard another sound, another rhythmic clink. I imagined another figure lifting, dropping, destroying, hoisting.

I moved toward the sound and thought that maybe it was a cop, or maybe one of the others—Jake or Sam or Edith—struck with the same idea. Then I wondered it if might be my father, a solitary form hammering away, helping me put the death-knell to this place. I stopped and smiled at this idea, imagined his taut back and broad shoulders covered in flannel, hoisting the red-handled pick axe that most nights rested on a hook above the garage workbench. I imagined how he'd look as I stepped up and joined him, stood at his side. He would give me a goofy, kidlike grin, like the ones he used to wear before *that night*—and put his arm around my shoulder.

"You wrecked this place," he would say, and then we would stand and destroy together.

But of course, when I got there, the sound was just the clinking of a piece of chain against a flagpole, jostled rhythmically by the wind. I surveyed the ground for a moment, disappointed. Dad was sitting home, pissed-off and waiting for me to sneak in the back door or to be led through the front, comforting Mom, and marinating the months' worth of icy glares and angry remarks that would be coming my way.

I took aim at the nearest building I could find and leveled the hammer, swung it until my arms were too spent to lift once more. Even then, I tried but it only lifted a foot off the ground before the muscles in my fingers failed altogether and the whole thing, handle and all, plunked harmlessly next to my sneaker. I never felt the pain until I stopped, but in that instant when I resolved my work was done, each finger, both palms, throbbed and ached with brutal force. Brick dust and concrete dust, and plain old dirt dust mixed with blood to coat my hands. My ribs, my back, my legs, my head—everything thrumped and ached. My fingertips tingled and would not stop; as much as I hated that feeling, I focused on it because in that moment, it was the least awful sensation I felt.

I wanted to keep the hammer with me as a sort of memento, but knew it wouldn't be allowed wherever I was headed when morning came. So I left it where it lay and once more scaled the fence. This time, each link tore into broken, encrusted hands—

but it was worthwhile excruciation. I left the mill grounds, crossed the street, and climbed the crumbling stairway up to the high school parking lot. The football stadium was unlocked, so I let myself in, and climbed the bleacher steps two at a time, to the press box and the flimsy ladder that took me up top.

I looked out at the dark field before me. This is where Dad had taken me the day after the plant closed. Longing for redemption or hope, a record crowd showed up to watch Wheelersburg run the score to 56-3 before their coach finally sent in his scrubs with three minutes left. Perched at our regular spot, bleacher seats 18 and 19 in Row G, overlooking the 40-yard-line, I sat next to my father and watched him weep like a baby. He tried like hell to kill those tears, wiping them away with a flannel sleeve. But the fly ash still on his sleeve just irritated his eyes and exacerbated the whole thing until I finally had to look away altogether, forcing myself to focus on the footballers sulking to the locker room. I tried to stare at girls in cheer skirts, at newspapermen popping off shots as fast as they could wind their film. Finally, I gave up the distractions and put my arm around Dad. It was the only time I ever saw him cry. And it was the saddest thing I've ever seen.

The night we took down the mill, I sat up there alone, waited for someone to come after me, watched for motion down below. I looked for signs that anyone really cared. I fell asleep waiting.

conventions

"And what does that make you?" asked the middle-aged woman in a pale yellow sweater when Bloomquist told her his name. Having never been keen on ancestry, he had no good answer to give so he stared straight forward and told her the same thing he'd said many times before in such situations: "I don't know *what* I am."

Where he was: a basement bar in Columbus, Ohio. Not even a hotel bar; he was still in the guts of the convention center (across the hall from a coffee shop and gift store, both with steel gates scrolled across their entrances). The young bartender had the look of someone who was allowed to close up shop and head home once these stragglers moved on, and he poured drinks in the same manner. Those stragglers, five of them including Bloomquist, had the looks of people who didn't much care.

Bloomquist was there because he preferred to linger over a drink rather than to hail a cab for the exurbs, rush back to his first floor economy hotel room with its iron bars across the windows. Excepting the basement bar, this neighborhood seemed barren of nightlife and he was well past the age, and short on the necessary motivation, to seek out some trendy nightspot uptown.

The yellow-sweatered woman laughed at his answer as if he'd said something terribly clever and then hailed the bartender. "I'll have bourbon and cola, please—go easy on the ice but not on the booze. Ha!" The bartender worked very hard to produce a smile, and he turned around to make the drink.

"What's that *you've* got?" the woman asked. "I'm Sherri, by the way. Did I say that already?"

She had. Twice.

"It's a—"

The bartender turned around and said dryly, "It's an appletini, ma'am."

"It's an appletini," Bloomquist repeated. When he'd arrived half an hour earlier, completely unsure what sort of drink he might like, he'd scanned the room and simply pointed to the most interesting looking thing in someone's hand. The bartender had raised his eyebrows as if the choice was odd, but nodded and said, "Coming up."

"So, Bloomquist, what is it you do?"

At home in Minneapolis, he would answer such questions with "computers" and people would be satisfied or even marginally impressed. Here though, at the convention, everyone did "computers." He would have to be more specific and the truth wasn't very sexy: what he did, concerning computers, was to sell over the telephone ink cartridges for printers that connected to them. More often than not, what he really did was call over the telephone people who had already bought products from his competitors' websites.

As he turned left and looked into Sherri's very large, very brown eyes, it occurred to Bloomquist that, so far from home, he could answer this question any way he liked. He could be anyone he chose—truth was irrelevant! He didn't *have* to tell her he was in computers, or even that he was part of the same convention. His nametag was safely tucked away, as was his company and title. The hall was large and segmented—surely other gatherings had taken place there today. In fact, there had been: the digital signboards had said so. For the briefest instant, he racked his brain. What had the other conventions been? That didn't matter, either. Sherri couldn't remember how frequently she'd said her own name; she'd never know who or what had convened in that great sprawling building. He smiled at this realization and took an extra-long sip from his drink to buy some thinking time.

He could tell her he was an astronaut! But then he looked down at the paunch of his belly, poorly hidden by the extra-large cardigan he wore over an Oxford cloth shirt—with just the slightest bit of fray beginning near the collar. Sure, John Glenn had gone into space at nearly eighty, but even that elderly man had a better physique than Bloomquist. No, she wouldn't believe that, not for one second.

He could say that he was an author, and a famous one, visiting town for a reading. The university was just down the street; he'd seen it on the way in. But then, she would ask his name, maybe ask him to scratch it down on one of the small cocktail napkins in the little wooden bin right in front of them. Then she'd take it home to the library or a bookstore and push the napkin across the counter and say, "I'd like to see one of this man's books!" and of course there wouldn't be any, and he certainly didn't want to make poor Sherri into a fool.

He could be a real estate agent, or a government man. A professional bowler, even, or an international trader! As all these ideas stumbled exuberantly about his head, his mouth said, "I'm in computers."

"Oh," she said. "That's wonderful. You must be here for the convention. I used to sell cable modems, but as you're quite aware, those went the way of dodo and dino, as my boss likes to say."

Bloomquist didn't know how to react to that, so he took another drink. Sherri's bourbon and cola was set in front of her and she hardly let the glass get flat on the bar before she swept it up and drank deeply. Bloomquist noticed that once the tumbler was in her hand, she didn't let it go. She held it close to her lips at all times, as if it were a thing whose escape she was intent on stopping. Her other elbow rested atop the bar with her hand elevated to eye-level, where she used her thumb to pick at the red polish of her other nails.

Sherri made short work of her drink, and the bartender flipped on the lights—all of them at once—a very unsubtle notification.

"Walk me to my hotel? It's very close, just down the street."

What Bloomquist wanted was to stay firmly planted on the barstool. The bartender's expression negated that possibility. What he wanted far less was to return to his motel and stare at the news by himself. He looked up at Sherri's overzealous smile, then at the bartender, who had turned his back, and then nodded that he would, indeed, go with her. He left cash on the bar and even held the door. The lock clicked behind them, and they laughed at their longevity.

Outside, Bloomquist looked up and saw the beginnings of a snowfall—a few flakes dropping slowly past the streetlights. With the streetscape all lit up still from Christmas, the scene would become so lovely once the snow came in earnest. When it did, he would tell Sherri how the city looked like a snow globe or diorama, and she would smile at his thoughtful observation.

But the snow never escalated to anything interesting—only drizzled enough to prime his face for the discomfort of a biting wind. He yanked at his collar to try and gain a bit more coverage, but it didn't help.

"Just a little farther," she told him for the third time. "Right up this street."

He mustered a smile but squinted, trying to make out anything ahead of them that resembled a hotel.

"Thank you again for walking me. I'm just not comfortable walking through cities alone, you understand."

"I understand," he said, but he didn't, really. This stretch of town seemed about one of the nicest yet dullest places he'd ever seen. It was well lit and he'd seen absolutely no one who might be considered menacing. He wanted to say this, but then, what he really wanted was to beg out, hail a cab, and go back to his room. As he began to run the evening through its possible conclusions, none of which seemed good, the ceiling cracks no longer seemed so bad, nor the news. But he said nothing and on they walked.

Four blocks later, they approached a dance club. Young men in torn-up jeans and dress shirts without ties stood with their arms folded, trying to act warm while young women—many in very short skirts and dresses—unabashedly shivered as they worked their way between velvet ropes, waiting to have their identification checked.

"Why, that looks fun," Sherri said.

No, it doesn't, Bloomquist thought, but he said, "I suppose it does."

"Like a fountain of youth!" She tugged on his arm. "Let's go—what do you say? Just for a bit. The hotel's only just up the road, but…"

"Sure." He was far more interested in the warm innards of the club than the experience. The thunderous, droning music was already giving him a headache, and they weren't even to the end of the line yet.

"You're so kind," Sherri said when the doorman took a token look at her date of birth. He didn't ask for Bloomquist's. Inside, Sherri ordered wine for both of them without asking.

"It's a nice Pinot!" she shouted over the music. He had no idea what that meant, and so he nodded and drank a bitter sip. He wanted his appletini back.

They stood along a wall for just a few moments, long enough to finish the Pinot. Bloomquist mostly stared at the ceiling but occasionally glanced at Sherri, who wore the look of someone who refused to admit how disappointed she was. It was not at all a fountain of youth, but rather a reinforcement of their age. Bloomquist could practically feel his own wrinkles vibrating with the steady, thudding pulse. Some kids waved glow sticks. Two young women began to kiss each other on a podium, while a crowd of boys crowed lurid words toward them.

What a terrible place she's brought me to, Bloomquist thought—and yet, he'd walked through the door, hadn't he?

"I'm tired," she finally said.

"Me too." They left. Further they walked, past tall buildings, across the interstate that trenched through the city's midsection. They walked and walked. His feet hurt, his knees ached, and he was sure she must have suffered similarly. Finally, she pointed off in the distance and said, "See, there it is!"

"It" was the Holiday Inn, with the neon letters H, L, and N non-functional, so that in the dark it actually read "oiday in."

She swiped her keycard three times before it worked, each attempt punctuated by a dramatic huff and an apologetic look, which turned into a smile, which bled into the next attempt. When the mechanism finally clicked, Bloomquist pulled the door open.

"May as well come in for a moment," she said. "Warm yourself up."

"I really shouldn't."

He looked down at the floor mat. It said, "Love."

He wondered why the floor mat would say such a thing.

She looked down at the ring on his left hand, shrugged, and said, "But that won't stop you."

He closed his eyes. Allowing for the difference in time zones, the children should just now be settling into bed. Was he supposed to call home? Probably, but he couldn't remember.

He followed her inside.

He sat on the desk chair, stained and faded, while she slipped off her clothes and left them in a pile on the filthy floor. He stared at the television, only saw her nudity reflected in the screen when it was particularly dark. Finally, she patted the mattress and said, "Come here, mister classy appletini man."

When Mrs. Bloomquist dropped him off at the airport, he had smiled and kissed her on the cheek. She kissed him on the cheek and then they kissed ever so briefly on the lips. It was their ritual in leaving, though it was Ellen Bloomquist who normally left. Bloomquist hadn't been to an out-of-town convention in years, but this time Marco had called in sick and Stevens was on vacation, Edward Jones had a brand new baby and Linda Walker was headed to a bigger expo in Seattle.

And so there, in full view of his flummoxed boss, Bloomquist had lifted his hand because he thought it might feel nice to be somewhere different for a few days. To be someone different, even. And Mr. Jenkins had shrugged and sent him off to the human resources office to file for an expense account, and that was that.

On the sidewalk outside the departures sign, Bloomquist stood with his black carry-on bag slung over his shoulder and he wondered how he ought to feel in a moment like this. He could feel excited and he could feel sad, he could feel nervous at the prospect of pitching items to real, live people and not just voices at the other end of the line. This trip could lead to great things! It could amount to nothing consequential. Before he selected an expression to wear, Ellen was in her car with the seatbelt fastened. She lifted her right hand in a small wave as soon as she had the car into gear and then she was gone and Bloomquist was alone.

Still, he stood there until another car pulled up and a man in a suit much trimmer than Bloomquist's rushed out of the back seat and nearly plowed over Bloomquist in the process.

"What's your problem?" the man yelled, and only then had Bloomquist shuffled through the automatic accordion doors and into the first of many lines. How many times had he done the same—pulled away from the curb with just the smallest of gestures toward his wife? She had never spoken a word of complaint. Perhaps she hadn't even stayed to watch—just walked straight through the doors without looking back at him. Bloomquist couldn't remember. But he could imagine that his wife must have been far more graceful in all of this. In leaving, in returning, in navigating the world. She would never have found herself straggling in the pit of the convention center's bar. She would never have needed to. Of that, Bloomquist was certain.

Had she ever been unfaithful during a trip? He wondered as he waited at the ticketing counter and the security line and the boarding gate, and then in the convention hall. Isn't that what people did at conventions?

When they finished, Sherri showered and he turned on the television, watched the sports scores first, then changed to a news report as she walked back into the room, her pale body wrapped in a stained white towel.

"Stay the night," she said. He shrugged and nodded that indeed, he would stay the night with Sherri from—where *was* she from? What did her name make *her*?

That's when the national news started. The bridge looked only mildly familiar when he saw it lying there, crumpled in the water, cars floating upside-down near the broken span. An aerial camera circled the wreckage. On the edges of the screen were the flashing lights of rescue vehicles, and he could make out people scurrying around on what was left of the bridge deck. The graphic on the screen said "Bridge Collapse—Dozens Killed, Others Missing" in bold letters. And then they showed a grainy video from someone's camera phone—the bridge full of cars; traffic moving slowly; the bridge wavering and then shrugging itself into the water. His face must've gone pale because Sherri asked him, "What is it, darling?"

"It's nothing," he said, and pulled his cell phone from his pocket and checked for messages and missed calls. Ellen crossed that bridge every day after picking up the children. She cursed sometimes about traffic at rush hour. She called him from that bridge so frequently to complain about traffic—on her way to it, on her way across it, on her way back from it. He looked again at the screen of his cell phone. Nothing. He dialed, placed an index finger over his lips so Sherri would keep quiet. It went straight to voicemail. She never turned her phone off, he knew, but perhaps it was simply filled with messages, all those people trying to check up on her. Perhaps she had turned it off to gain a moment's peace. That was it—she must be sleeping. She must be.

Bloomquist settled back onto the mattress without trying the home line. It would be unkind to wake them up, he decided, and that certainly wasn't the kind of person he was. Sherri slipped into bed. "I'm so very glad I met you," she said. "You seem like such a wonderful man."

He wished, as she curled against him, that he'd chosen a far more interesting thing to be.

miss ellen told me

She hadn't been gone even an hour when they came knocking at my door with their notepads and questions. I sat there on my sofa for a solid minute without budging, just sat and thought it all through because I knew what they were going to ask, and there were two ways to go about answering—two truths I could tell. I picked the one I did because of this: even worse than the sight of all those armed men pulling her from her doorway was the way those news vans with their Fayette County plates lined up along Shady Fork Lane, parked in the middle of the street, on lawns, in my driveway—all without asking a soul's permission because they were the *news* and because they *could*. So on the sixth knock or so I finally pushed myself up out of the sofa and took a step, but even then I checked myself and picked up the Mason jar off my coffee table and took it with me, the liquid inside instantly warming my hand.

I made myself look good and somber when I opened up.

"Can I help y'all?"

I drew this out because I know how gleeful people with cameras get over making folks look backward when things like this happen.

A man with slicked-down black hair stepped to the front.

"We were wondering if you could tell us anything about Miss Yelena—"

"Oh—" I said, as if shocked. As if I couldn't predict every last contrived question. "You mean Miss *Ellen*." He tried to correct me and I looked at him in such a way that he quit mid-sentence.

I stepped outside into full view of those cameras and left my door hang open as I said exactly what everyone says when his neighbor makes the news for some awful reason: "She was just a sweet old lady, nothing but lovely, and she always waved when she walked the dog, and none of us could imagine her doing such things, and it just breaks a person's heart to hear how brutal it'd all been." When I quit, the reporters kept scribbling to catch up, but they seemed satisfied, some of them even grinning like the syrup that had just dripped off my lips was going to win them a writing prize. Then, just before the first cameraman reached toward the red button that would shut off his machine, I opened my mouth again and said one last thing, the most truthful thing I said that whole day. I said, "She even had me over for tea," and I held up my jar, took a fair sized pull from it.

Then the cameras did shut off. The reporters and all the neighbors who spent that afternoon milling around and shaking their heads in disbelief looked at me and said, "Awww, poor thing." and one of the lady reporters even gave me a hug, like I'd said something real sentimental. Then she patted me on the back and told me to watch Channel Seven Action News at 5:30 and 11. I didn't bother telling her I don't keep a television at my place.

Now, old Tad Stephens from down the road, I heard he told the reporters it couldn't have been Miss Ellen at all, that they'd come after the wrong lady altogether, and that they'd release her as soon as they checked the fingerprints and realized the mistake. In no time, he said, she'd be back to that creaky old porch swing in front of her mobile home, waving to passers-by, as was her God-given right. (You can hardly say a thing in Lee County without associating God, as if God gives some sort of damn about porch swings.) Didn't Tad look ridiculous, though, when the DNA tests came back a perfect match? Didn't he look a fat, blue fool when the extradition papers were signed and she was flown right to Sarajevo on that big green U.S. Army plane? The picture of that plane leaving the Bluegrass Airfield was in all the newspapers.

•

Something was off kilter from the first day she moved in. That spring afternoon, I watched through the slats of my blinds, held a finger-width apart, when a black car with no license plates dropped her. She carried just a few things, bedding and cookware and such. All of it seeming brand new, still in packaging. That just wasn't right for an old lady: her things should be familiar and well worn. Afghans and family photos and the like, not a couple of boxes fresh off the shelf. It just didn't add up. And then with no hug from the driver—the driver never even got out!—the car tore off with the speed of someone who knew just how much gas to give on those hills. Left her there in the loneliest bend of Johnson Hollow. She got left right where no one would probably ever find her, which made me think she was real heavily invested in not being found.

Every now and then that black car came back, but for the most part she just walked around the place on her own. She started a good-sized garden, and it wasn't cute hobbyist stuff like spices, but meal foods like tomatoes and potatoes and squashes and some of the tallest corn I've ever seen a person grow. She mowed her lawn by hand with one of those squeaking roller contraptions they sell at antique stores and she concentrated heavily on keeping the ditchline low, something the Penningers before her were wont to do. This gained my favor instantly. She washed her windows every few days, inside and out—real thorough—with a bucket and cloth. I would've offered to lend a hand in some of this except she seemed so happy doing all that work, so purposeful.

•

The mill is only a mile or so down the street, but that's a long way for a 60-year old woman. That was the other thing, too—what business did she have working full-time, and with such intensity? Surely a woman that age should've had some savings, or some inheritance or a pension or something. But she just hoofed it to work, early without fail. When I realized we were on the same shift, I offered to drive her, and she just smiled a big smile with all those gaps where teeth used to be, and she shook her head and said she needed to keep her strength up. And I kept my mouth shut and wondered what for.

Now, I know folks talk all sorts of ways, so I didn't think twice about the accent. I really didn't. (She didn't say much, besides.) But all these little things didn't add up to anything normal, and I thought of them daily while I worked across the line from her, each of us planing timber for dressers and shelving units and all sorts of hideous furniture that got sorted and packed by high school part-timers who'd come after we cleared out for the evening. Once, I looked up at her and made a joke about what ugly furniture we made, and she glared at me across the machinery so hard I thought my heart might stop. So I backtracked and said, "Maybe it's not really that bad after all," and she said "Only the weak complain about work," and I told her how right she was. The rest of the day, I held the boards even tighter when feeding them through the planer so she wouldn't see how my fingers shook. I realized that day I was terrified of the little old woman across the street.

Most of the time she kept her head down and worked, and I swear I've never seen another human go about business with such furious, precise movement. How she held each board in exactly the same way. The firmness of her motion. The rhythmic, careful cadence of her breathing. The absolute focus of her eyes.

Before long, I sensed she could see the wheels turning in my head, putting two and two together. She knew I was different from those other guys at the mill who just silently swung their arms over and over again. That must be why one day she looked up at me and said, "Richard, you'll come have tea with me tonight." It was the most grandmotherly she'd ever seemed, the least forced I ever saw her smile.

I've never been one for tea. Since back in high school I've been a bourbon man through-and-through, with Budweiser next and then maybe coffee. But the way she spoke it was pretty clear this was no question, but a commandment. And who was I to say no to a sweet old lady, even if I expected she wasn't nearly as sweet as she was old.

To top it all off, she even let me drive her home that evening—*asked* me to do it. It was getting on to autumn and the sun had been setting earlier and earlier and it was gloomy that day to begin with so I suppose she figured it wouldn't hurt to be off the road just that once. I dropped her off at her door, told her I'd go change out of my work clothes. She just nodded.

When I came back across the street on foot, she stood on the porch, still wearing her blue company shirt and work denim, peering out at the street. The front door was propped open with a little wedge of cut wood. Inside was a small table and a pair of chairs, both fashioned of polished timber. "Did you make these?" I asked. She nodded so slightly that I wondered if her face had even moved or just her eyebrows, then she gestured for me to sit at the one nearest the door, the one with its back to the door. She kicked away the doorstop, glanced left and right, then pulled it tight and cranked the deadbolt.

Candles lit the room. There wasn't even a light fixture overhead, just raw wires drooping from a round hole cut in the drywall. The candles were different heights and colors, resting all over the place: on the floor, on a rickety wood crate near the door, on shelves. She had about a dozen of them flickering on the square kitchen table (which looked handmade, too), along with an open box of Domino sugar, a teaspoon jabbed deep into it. "Hello," she said, and I said hello back, and she walked off into the kitchen. As soon as she left the room, a teakettle started to whistle, as if she'd known exactly the moment to fetch it. She came back with a steaming kettle and two mismatched mugs— mine was off-white with the smallest chip out of its handle and hers was deep blue. The tea wasn't in bags like I'd seen it before, but dropped right down inside the mug, and she poured water over the top (mine first) so that little slivers of dried leaves and berries came to the surface. "Sugar?" she asked, but she'd already dumped two spoonsful into my drink before she was done asking. I nodded, even though I never take sugar in my coffee and I was pretty sure I wouldn't take it with tea, either. I had to admit to myself, though, that it did smell pretty nice. Not very manly. Not the sort of thing I'd drink on my own. But it smelled sweet and fragile, like just the right thing to drink with her—like the drink stood in for a part of her that was missing. She picked up her mug first and said, "Like this," then sipped at it with her lips tight so just a little tea got sucked through and the leaves stayed out of her mouth. I tried, and drank half the leaves in one sip. She shook her head and didn't really smile, but turned up the left corner of her lip like she was giving it a good effort. "You'll learn," she said before returning to her own mug and sipping carefully once more.

She watched me sip, her eyes wide and cool looking—not angry by any stretch, but quite cool. Much better, she said the second time I sipped and she nodded again in her slight way as if I'd passed a test.

And then, she told me.

She told me her real name, Yelena. She told me how dearly she missed wearing her pressed green blouse with its thin chevrons and insignia, her name etched into a small tag attached above the right breast pocket. She drew it out for me, in pencil, right on the table: Елена, and then traced it again with her chipped and yellowed fingernail.

"Mill workers look so shabby in their drooping work clothes," she said. She looked away, through the wide-open window. This time, she didn't look like she was keeping watch, but trying to bring something back. As she stared off at the tree line, I saw a new hardness in her eyes, a coldness that allowed me to believe her without the slightest question when, seconds later, she told me how she killed all those people, how she ran the steel of her blade across their throats, how she sometimes held their hands while she did it so she could feel their response to her cut. How her unit was comprised of women who disguised themselves in Albanian or Kosovar clothing so that they could sneak into towns and camps, right into homes and tents without anyone becoming the least bit suspicious until it was far too late and the knives were drawn and moving so quickly. How their faces would twist and their chests would heave in failed attempts to breathe as they desperately tried to vomit up the gasoline she made them drink. So they'd know they were inhabiting land that was not theirs. So they'd know they had sinned against nature and against Serbia, that they did not deserve to live. How she would kill all day long without wiping her blade so that it would retain the blood of every last enemy, each interloper—the male soldiers and the KLA wives, the sad children and frail old ones alike—and would then soak the knife at night in a jar of hot water until the blood dissolved and turned the fluid a rich, deep brown. How she would drink it like tea—slowly, so that she could taste every emptied heart. How, when the drink was finished, she would sharpen and polish the weapon so that it would be ready for morning's killing. I was so caught up in the words, it took me a moment to realize she was physically rubbing her right hand over her left, demonstrating how she moved to clean her instrument. She had been acting the whole thing out, showing me the movements, teaching me. I felt the blood run from my head and I took another quick drink from the mug to keep myself from reacting or speaking, or thinking too much on it all. I drank fast, and I drank deep, and I didn't even purse my lips, didn't try to keep the floating matter from my mouth.

She told me how they carried almost no supplies, and instead took what they needed as they moved. "Guerillas," she said, and her accent became sharper—truer—when she said that, like she relished the sound of it. She repeated the word and nodded, then told me how she even used that knife on her own soldier once, one night when a woman from her band of raiders grew slothful in her movement, loud and slow, lagging behind the others.

"You'll be the death of us!" Miss Ellen shouted, and the sound echoed off the walls of her home. "That's what I told her, and she wept. I told her to stop—one, two, three times, and still she wept, so—" Miss Ellen ran the tip of her index finger left-to-right across the base of her neck, slowly tracing her own clavicles.

"You—"

She smiled and nodded, then continued. She described it all so clearly that I never doubted her for an instant. Never doubted a tiny detail of it. That voice rang so low and so sweet that I wasn't even afraid of her. Can you imagine? That would have been the natural reaction—to fear her, to wonder if that knife was hiding in her blouse right then and there, *waiting*. For me! She'd killed her own soldier—who was *I*? It should have occurred to me that she would have no qualms about murdering me once she finished tattling on herself (and how good it must have felt to let it out). But I just sat and listened, and the more gruesome her story grew, the more relaxed and kindly she seemed. She quit gesturing and settled back into her chair, growing less enthusiastic but seeming more contented. Wistful. The more relaxed she grew, the more I settled back into my own seat.

"All those Kosovars, acting as though the land was theirs and not Serbian," she said. "Like they belonged there." She talked faster and faster. She shed that moment of calm like an uncomfortable skin and built back up, her hands slowly balling into fists. She told me about those "greedy louses, walking around cocksure of themselves." Of course, she said, they had to go, had to be driven away. And when they wouldn't leave— that's when Miss Ellen's unit went to work. (She stayed Miss Ellen to me—Yelena was the person who did these things, of course, not the one who told me about them.) It occurred to me in the middle of her explanation that maybe I should be thinking something fearful or accusatory as she talked, but that dropped quickly out of mind when she started to talk about meeting with General Slobodan (because that's a name I remembered from the news) and I forgot about right and wrong, focused instead on the fame of the man who told her to show no mercy to those wretched thieves and gypsies and traitors. Then she slammed down her fist on the table and stood up, quickly, reverently before repeating his words: "If they will not leave our land," she shouted, "they must leave this earth!" She sat down again and breathed and smoothed out her work shirt. Some sawdust fell out of the fabric folds. She rubbed her hands together and looked disgusted and I couldn't tell if it was over the dust or the work clothes or something else altogether. But then she looked at me and the hint of a smile formed and she very quietly told me how her band of lady soldiers stalked through village after village looking for others to exterminate. Miss Ellen told me about the villages, all those exotic town names, all the places where she intruded, and the nights camping at the edges of cliffs or deep inside forests, in cave mouths even. "The sadness was great," she said, "when we found a town already smoking, the people gone. When a bomb or other soldiers beat us to the glory. It was failure." As she said all this, I had this image playing through my mind where she moved like Sherman through the south except quieter and madder and more hateful. She looked directly into my eyes, as if she was reading me as she spoke. "I was even more disappointed," she said, "When we found empty houses, when we found the belongings left behind by another family of weaklings who fled. Who chose to become refugees." She sighed and then her voice lost half its volume and grew sullen. "My teas were paler those nights, and I drank them quicker, with disappointment."

She sipped again from her cooling drink, and I did the same, entranced, enticed, compelled to follow her lead. She slipped into her native language then, something that sounded like a prayer, and she tilted her head upward but closed her eyes as she whispered the words. "It was my duty," she said, "and I loved to fulfill my duty."

"Has it happened...since you've been here?" I asked. "I mean, in Kentucky."

She sat back in her chair and squinted and her irises seemed to flicker, sort of the way you can see a camera lens focusing when someone has it pointed at you. Those eyes, I could almost feel them pushing deep through to the back of my head. And then, with forcefulness that seemed to surprise even her, she said, "I have no such duty here." She looked so sad after she said that, and she didn't speak for a moment, just looked at the wall and then at the table. She dug at a loose splinter in the table with her fingernail, then sighed. I imagined at first that sadness came from her being so far away from home, from being lost, fleeing like the people she despised. But something told me it wasn't that at all—it was just that she missed the killing. That she missed feeling so useful. As I thought all of this, she leaned forward, rested both forearms on the table, and then she let those eyes open all-the way, like the little camera she had in there had just shot its picture and she was letting all the light back in.

"Would you like to see it?"

"See what?"

"Of course you would, of course you would!" and she stood up with snap-quick reflex and grabbed one of the candles and she was out of the room in a blink. I leaned forward so I could watch around the doorframe. There she was hunched over with her back toward me, removing a loose floorboard then reaching down. When she pulled it up, the candlelight bounced off it and I saw the thing gleam like Arthur's sword. All the muscles in her hands tensed up the way she held on so tight, more firmly than she'd ever grasped a plank at work, using every bit of her strength to hold and protect it. She held it out in front of her and turned it over, and of course at this point I stopped leaning and sat straight in my chair so she wouldn't know I'd been watching.

Miss Ellen walked back into the room with her palms facing up and the knife resting across them. She held it out for me. "Go ahead," she said. "Hold it. Take it into your hand." I didn't take it from her, but I ran my finger across the blade. It was so cold at first touch that it almost seemed hot, and she smiled her big toothless smile, and said, "I know, I know how you feel, child." She placed the knife on the table and went right back to her tea, and I couldn't take my eyes off it. I couldn't stop wavering back and forth between thinking how terrible it was to have the thing sitting so close to me, and how strangely gorgeous it was, that arced line of smooth, shining steel.

•

She never spoke of any of it again. Not the knife or Yelena or her home. She never spoke another word to me about anything that happened outside of Lee County. She never again invited me to tea, or to come visit, or to help her till or plant that spring, and even though I know it shouldn't have, I suppose that made me a little sad. I mean, there she was, the sort of person they make movies about, or shows on the History Channel, living right across the street from me. It wasn't so much that I needed to know more, but I wanted to hear her *tell* it again. That's not the sort of thing you bring up over cups of coffee in the break room, though.

•

When they brought her out of the house that humid afternoon, cuffed and guarded, she looked straight at me, and I wondered if she thought it was me who told. But she smiled and tried to lift her weathered old hand to wave. One of the soldiers—some punk teen—smacked her needlessly with the butt of his rifle and she dropped her head and that was the last I saw of those hard old eyes. They pushed down on her head and shoved her through the door, and I turned away because I'd seen flat enough of it. I sat on my sofa and practiced being surprised as I waited for the news trucks to turn up.

•

It feels strange to look up from my work and see someone else standing across the planer from me. And every few days, it *is* someone else—always seems like it's someone new. Lenny and Allen got their pink slips the other day, latest in a long line. They wouldn't cut their salary in half is what I hear, though that sort of thing can get exaggerated sometimes, and it's just as likely they were stealing and the boss let them off with their dignity. Jonny, though, he just gave up, said he wasn't going to be pushed out, gave his two weeks. I'm still hanging in there, but I wonder how long I've got, how long it'll be before I'm called into the office. The guys across from me come and go now, and they don't speak, except to each other in the break room, and I can't tell a damn word they're saying. They just stand in there and carry on like they belong. I've worked that line 18 years, and they don't even nod in the morning before we work. They just ignore me, talk to each other like I'm the intruder. The boss sent around a memo that said we "should learn to communicate better," and put a book in the break room: Instant Spanish. They accused *me* of tearing it up, but I told them the truth: "I wouldn't even touch it to tear it in half." I imagine Jonny tore it up before he threw in the towel, but I didn't say so—wouldn't welch on him any more than I did on Miss Ellen. It would've been no use, anyway. Some days I don't even go in there anymore it makes me so aggravated—being ignored, I mean. Frank, the shift boss, sometimes introduces the new hires, but no one pays much attention, especially to the names because sometimes a guy will be Ernesto and he'll work a few weeks then disappear for a month (to some other plant, I imagine) and then he'll come right back when Frank posts a wage increase in the paper, except now he's Diego or Pablo, and everyone in the place knows it, but no one says anything because the labor's cheap and from the sound of it the plant's just barely hanging on and I guess at some level they think this is better for everyone. So people come and they go and no one can keep any sort of track and they get paid in cash while I still get that same old check with a tax-dent chunked out of it, and I don't know how anyone would even find out if one went missing. And every morning it's a new person or a new name across from me, and we ignore each other and go to work; all the while I'm thinking about Miss Ellen, and I wonder how if this was how she felt at the very beginning when all those new people with strange eyes and shifting names started appearing and disappearing.

•

I wanted to check right away, but I waited a couple weeks before I risked going over there, and even then I went at night and took a flashlight, one of those little ones that slide into your pants pocket. It was a Thursday, almost midnight, and I shut off my own houselights and then walked slow as can be down my driveway and then up hers. I figured I'd have to break a window or something, but the door handle turned and I went right in. I shut the door behind me in case someone drove by and got suspicious, then I got on my hands and knees and fished the flashlight from my pocket, flipped it on and kept it pointed low. From what I could tell crawling across the floor, everything was just as it'd been, like the only thing that changed was the sun went down. I'd expected the place to be torn up, but I guess they had all the evidence they needed back in Europe. In the kitchen, I felt around until I found a loose floorboard.

•

Sometimes I drive over to the public library and hand over my card so I can use one of the computers to look up her name. No one thinks a thing of it: her names (both of them) are in the search history on every one of those Hewlett Packards. Everyone wants to know more about her. Type in the first three letters, Y-E-L, and the screen fills up with lists of places to find pictures and articles and histories, all the links already turned a different color from somebody else's clicking. And so I sit down and read the stories, and see the pictures of her in olive drab looking cold and ruthless, defiant. (In one of the photos, you can even see the knife handle sticking out from her belt!) I search to see if there's any news about what's happened to her, though I have a good idea it was nothing pleasant. I imagine that in the end, someone probably cut her neck the same way she did to all those other people, and whoever held the knife probably enjoyed it just as much as she had. I force myself to read once more the lists of crimes she committed—and confessed to me, right there at her hand-made table. I wonder if she told the story herself at trial, or if she listened to the prosecutor list all her deeds while she smiled (or tried not to on the advice of her lawyer). I read about how all the people she killed were civilians. Women and children mostly, terrified and unarmed. And how those people were really citizens of the country, and that she walked into their homes and slashed them all up to bits. A demon. That's what she was, I tell myself: a demon, through-and-through. I read the whole story and tell myself that she's pure evil, that it's a blessing for Commonwealth and country to be rid of such a monster.

But by the time I get home, all those newsprint words have faded and all I can think of is how she was just the little old lady who lived across the street, who rocked on that porch swing and didn't bother a soul. None of the computers have Miss Ellen in the search history, after all, and that's what she was to me. When I pull into my driveway, the shabby For Sale sign in front of that dilapidated place makes me sad, and I know no one will probably ever want it again, on account of its reputation. I think about trimming the ditchline or tending to the garden so the place doesn't look eerie and empty. But instead, I turn my own door handle and go to the kitchen. Now, I don't know where one buys the sort of tea that's dumped right into a mug, but I did find a yellow carton full of Lipton bags down at the IGA in Galesburg. So when I get home from those library trips and I'm thinking about Miss Ellen I reach up into my cabinets and pull down the box of Lipton and set some water on the stove. I don't have a proper mug, so I take a Mason jar, a good clear one, and I put the teabag down in the bottom, along with some sugar cubes because it turns out that I *do* like sugar with my tea. When the kettle whistles (I always wait for it to whistle even when I can hear the water boiling first) I pour the water into that glass jar, over top of the teabag, and I get down on my knees and push aside the little rug that covers a floorboard I made loose on my own, and I pull up one plank and reach my arm down into the darkness and even though I don't look my hand always knows how to find the spot right away. Despite the way it's sitting there on the bare stone of my home's foundation I never wash it, never rinse it off, and I rest it next to the jar and wonder how it would feel to dip it inside and churn the liquid as those broken pieces of leaf turn the boiled water a rich, deep brown.

abigail newton goes to church alone again

The smiling man at the coffee bar is attentive and careful as he pours pumpkin spice flavored coffee but he's got a gold ring already and when she smiles back, it's not her best work. Let's be straight here: Abigail Newton is lonely as hell, and for the past six months she's tried to forget that fact, week by week, in all the places that might possibly make her feel more celestial. The newest repair is a four-story palace of steel and glass and coffee bars and flat panel televisions, a place that's got nearly everything she wants this morning—if it weren't for all the wedding bands and backpack babies.

Abigail Newton does not have children, though she's occasionally borrowed children from friends and cousins—under the rouse of babysitting, of course—for the purpose of meeting single fathers in the sorts of places single fathers might be but where 36-year-old childless women have no particular business loitering: playgrounds and kiddie amusement parks and miniature golf courses, bike trails and dog parks and even baseball games. Each of these attempts has ended in some blend of fiscal deficit, ringing ears, strained muscles, and line after line of mental field notes on the construction and tendencies of complete, functional families. The way they communicate in glances, the way they negotiate and grimace, scold and then smile—the undulation of it all.

"Glad you've come to worship with us today, ma'am," the coffee pourer says as he pushes the drink toward her. There's a little twang to it and it feels forced, like it's a part of the evangelical uniform he's obliged to wear. Abigail Newton could do without the pretense. She could *really* do without the twang. In terms of content, though, he feels exceptional for a moment. He's spoken to her with more depth and detail than any who passed through the queue before her. But then she realizes she's just daydreaming again, and that she's holding up the line.

Abigail says, "Glad to be here." And she is.

The church lobby looks and feels very much like a shopping mall, and since it's still half an hour out from the service time she's decided to attend, she does what people do in places that feel like shopping malls: Abigail Newton roams.

First she roams to the ladies' room to examine her hair and examine the light film of her makeup, the shape of that hard line between lipstick and skin, to make certain that everything is in its prime state. She even adjusts the straps of her sundress—yes, yes, everything is in place. Nothing is in need of further adjustment. She pauses, though, in this otherwise empty room, places her hands on the sink counter and shuts her eyes to pray. It's not lost on her that this is perhaps the only part the building where this particular act seems out of place, and yet it's maybe the most private spot, so there might even be some merit, a logic to this odd location. She doesn't pray for anything in particular, because she's tried a thousand strands of specificity already at a thousand volumes and in a hundred different postures. She's prayed with the Methodists for greater faith and for serenity and with the Baptists for love and for something to distract her from the absence of love and with the Catholics for patience and for ambition. She's prayed with the Presbyterians for wisdom and discernment and even with the Anglicans for recklessness and the ability to quit caring altogether. She's asked for all these things in turn. Maybe some of these things even came to her in fashions and spurts, but if those prayers were ever answered, the solutions came too subtle for her noticing and never gave her anything but a variant shade of hollow. What she asks for now is just general goodness. For something hopeful to happen. A simple burning bush or two.

Finished, Abigail Newton wanders back beneath all those skylights, behind all those glass doors. If this were a movie treatment, a single beam of light would follow her, perhaps aimed by a guardian angel with fantastic hair, clothed in skinny jeans and a knowing grin. He would be some combination of mischievous or novice. Or perhaps hers would be once fallen and now ascendant. Either way, they would guide her to the answer, which would come in the form of a smiling man and a nice house, maybe even an uptick in occupation. That guardian angel would ferry her all the way through to the playful montage, scored with dance songs from the eighties until a fade-to-black, perfectly timed to insinuate a perfectly happy future.

But Abigail Newton's life is no film.

She wanders across the atrium, dotted with pole-mounted television monitors that show inklings of the service going on right now, a duplicate of which she'll soon experience in the flesh. It feels as though there might be an Auntie Anne's and a Limited on the mezzanine, if the second level weren't a daycare. She sits and sips at her coffee, which she's topped with just a touch of cream and a touch of sugar. She doesn't particularly care for either, but the ways in which a person prepares a drink can be a great conversation starter, and to the best of her knowledge, no one's ever started a life-changing conversation by talking about black coffee, even if there was pumpkin spice flavor brewed into it.

After a moment of sipping, she thinks better of her seat choice and scales one of the grand stairways toward the row of barstools that line the balcony. She looks down at where she's just been, and watches as a well-dressed man (he's even got a nice, classic wristwatch with a black leather band) who appears to be in his late twenties maneuvers into the very seat she just vacated.

Figures.

If she were anywhere else, she would curse between her teeth.

But there are empty seats next to her, available for someone social, someone like her who doesn't wish to be confined by the isolation of a table.

This is the kind of church where people look each other up in the missed connections section of Craigslist afterward. It could be a city street at 5:05 p.m., but with no traffic lights and fewer people asking for money. People buzz around and smile, say fast hellos and then flit onward. She surveys the room and smiles and tells herself that this is a place where possibility can start. As the thought formed, she was acutely aware that it sounded more like a corporate slogan than the trajectory of her evening. She thinks it again and decides her new slogan has no meaning whatsoever. She takes a sip of coffee and returns to watching.

Before the doors open for the next service, the earlier thousands leave through their own set of doors. They churn and braid beneath her like a tankful of guppies: some headed straight for the door and their spot at a restaurant table, perhaps in front of a screen with a game. Others go back for coffee refills before they leave, or mingle with friends or stand in line to pick up children. Some rush. Some loiter. When they're gone, the doors remain closed for a while—presumably while the stage is reset. She waits at the door: Abigail Newton is about to play the seat lottery. She will find a row of her own and leave it to providence.

She has been known to cheat at the seat lottery. More than once, when flanked with grandmothers or prototypical, full families, she's accepted a fake phone call as an excuse to vacate the spot and try again. Today, with so many people vying for seats, she might not have that chance. She'll have to pick wisely.

There is a small beep that accompanies the timed opening of the automatic doors. It may as well be a starting gun. Abigail Newton walks slowly enough to ensure she doesn't spill coffee on herself, but she is the first one through her door and the first one to claim a spot in a side section, six rows from the stage. It is an unpretentious spot, one where a thoughtful person of superior hygiene and speckled morals might sit.

Instead, two teenagers take the seats directly to her left and play games on their phones. Perhaps there's a father who will collect them. She takes out her own phone and finds excuses to fiddle with it, to seem occupied. When she looks up, the kids are gone and she's mercifully alone again in the row: she's gotten a reprieve, a chance for an upgrade.

Abigail Newton sets her cup of coffee in the drink holder and waits. Her heart ticks a little quicker every time someone approaches her row. She makes sure to rest her left hand on her left knee, her naked ring finger in clear view of any potential row neighbors. She turns and glances at the aisle, filled with a steady stream of parishioners. Already, she anticipates defeat. Already, she's thinking about how she will navigate her own exit when the time comes.

She smiles. People smile back. She says hello a few times, even, and each time, it feels like an inflated balloon is trying to escape her throat. Abigail wants to find a positive insinuation in this, but everyone knows inflated balloons do primarily two things: float away and burst.

She finishes her coffee. Her row is still empty. The countdown clock behind the pastor's microphone boasts of seven minutes and thirty-six seconds until the service starts, while reminding families to deposit their children in the nursery. She panics. She bails out. Or maybe, she just needs more caffeine. Out into the aisle, she salmons against the oncoming masses, races to the coffee line and stands and stands and stands, the brown paper insulator soaking up just some of the clamminess from her palm. This time, she takes plain black coffee grown at an Ethiopian collective, and she supposes she'll take a little creamer, even though it seems like the destruction of a fine thing. She walks back into the auditorium and is tempted to sit in the darkened back rows, the way they had in those in-between years—when she and her sister were young and they hadn't quit going to services altogether but her mom had gotten good and tired of answering questions about where Joe was and when he'd be coming back to join in the worshipping.

Again she moves toward the front, underneath the stage light rigging and with a clear view of one of the large stadium screens. But not too close to the bank of fog machines—she's got an inkling they inflect her allergies. Row thirteen is, somehow, still entirely empty and she chooses the center seat. Someone will have to sit by her.

There are still three minutes left, but a video has begun—something akin to the movies, reminding people to turn off their phones. She remembers sitting at her mother's hip and watching how the minister would come down from behind his pulpit and lecture children for speaking or rustling in their seats; now, it's just a suggestion that your phone doesn't go off. She's not sure which way she prefers. She's not sure what that says about her.

"This taken?"

She shakes her head and tries not to look disappointed as a family of seven shuffles into her row. But there's still the other side—until four college boys sidestep their way in toward her, still whispering about last night's exploits, something between cackles about getting their money's worth out of this week's forgiveness. They leave a gap seat, though—one empty space left.

The lights dim and the band starts. Abigail Newton stands to sing, and she does so beautifully—or at least she imagines so. It feels nice to be drowned out by the wall of sound that descends upon her. For even her loudest of joyful noises to do nothing more than blend into the room and waft toward the rafters. At the end of the song, a lady reads a list of announcements and asks everyone to move in, to get rid of the spare spaces so there's room for everyone. The college boy nearest Abigail looks at her and half-smiles, but stays right where he is.

And then: an usher comes to her row, flashlight blazing. It's almost time to pray, but perhaps this time the answer has come first. The usher is escorting a young man with tortoiseshell glasses and an undercut and a cardigan, and the usher brings this man directly to Abigail's row, spots his flashlight on the seat next to her (yes, in film treatment fashion), and everyone's about to stand so it'll be easy for him to get through and it won't be awkward at all, and he's even gotten there before the part where everyone shakes hands and meets their neighbor and—at the end of the row, a woman takes the liberty of waving everyone down a seat. The most reluctant of the hung-over students finally slides toward her and that beautiful, perfect man remains out there on the edge, so near but so critically unreachable.

"Amen," she hears. The word reverberates through the tremendous sound system and she's missed everything that preceded it. "Amen," she whispers, because that's the word for endings inside this building.

And so the service begins in earnest, and Abigail Newton listens to a minister talk about carving out room for personal time in a world of over-connectivity. The boys to her right and the family to her left nod frequently, and are kind enough to avoid staring when she gives up on trying to keep her sighs inaudible.

"Hey there, beautiful!"

She stops in her tracks, there in the middle of the lobby.

That balloon sensation appears in Abigail's throat. She turns. Slowly.

A man who's just fetched his kids is waving down his wife, who happens to stand just on the other side of Abigail.

There's a third thing that balloons do: deflate slowly until they're hollow and past usefulness. Abigail feels the air leave her lungs, and when she continues breathing, she can't tell for sure whether they're actually filling again. She simply stands there, unable to move. She imagines she hears the undulation of voices, feels the churning and braiding of the crowd around her. In the aquarium full of guppies, Abigail Newton is the plaster coral.

Abigail Newton fetches one more coffee. This time, she skips the flavoring, skips the cream, skips the sugar, takes her drink the way she wants it. The door-holding greeters gone, she pushes her own way through the West Lobby Exit. She practically jogs to her green Volkswagen, buckles her seatbelt, and gets in line to leave, traffic belayed by a bearded youth and then a tall woman and then an elderly man, each waving aircraft control wands to send everyone to an appropriate exit.

If Abigail Newton would look at her rearview mirror, she would see the vehicle behind her, a recently washed black sedan driven by the man with tortoiseshell glasses and a cardigan and an undercut. It's just as well that she doesn't look up, because nothing rational can be done about it now anyway.

Abigail Newton places her name on the list for a brunch table. On the waiting bench—too uncomfortable to make up for the spectacular aging that marks its wood grains—she sips complementary black coffee from a foam cup. Cream and sugar are not an option.

As she waits for the host to call out for *Newton, party of one*, she takes her phone from her pocket and turns it back on. She navigates to recent pages, selects the missed connections section of Craigslist and presses refresh and sips and presses refresh and sips and takes her table.

"What can I get for you, ma'am?" asks the waiter, and she doesn't look up from the menu to see what he looks like or what he is or isn't wearing on his finger.

She mumbles that she'd like the French toast with bourbon maple glaze and he's not sure if he heard it, so he leans closer and asks her to repeat, so she does. He pours her a coffee on his next pass by—before she even asks.

When the food comes, she presses refresh and then bites into it and swears that she'll only press refresh this once more and then get on with her day. The smiling waiter asks her if she's got everything she needs and she thinks about that for a moment, but he's busy and he walks off and he spares her taking a definitive stance, so she takes another bite and presses refresh once more.

basement party

My hair was still dripping from a rushed shower after basketball practice and the last thing I wanted to do was step out into the cold. But Dad steered into a divey old convenience store near the neighborhood where he grew up and shifted into park with the kind of finality that said I'd better not try and keep parked in my seat. I'd expected at least a talk along the way: I was minutes away from my first basement party, and as he sidled up to the counter and ordered for us I figured it could be worse. The talk couldn't get too graphic or uncomfortable out there in broad public view.

When our vanilla milkshakes were ready, we sat at the only table, right up against the front window. Instead of the birds and the bees, though, he told me about how he used to sit there with his father, a man I'd met just once—on my birthday. They'd carried me across the hospital to the cancer wing and put me in his arms, snapped a quick picture. It was the first one of me, and the last one of him. His dad couldn't afford milkshakes, but bought them from time to time. An excuse to sit with his kid. The talk didn't touch me the way it was meant to, I guess. The third time he caught me looking at my watch, he quit sucking on his straw and reached across the table to pat my shoulder.

"It's good to be a little late," he said. "Trust me."

•

I knocked feebly as I stood in front of the door, backlit by Dad's headlights in the driveway so that my shadow looked like it was plastered to the door panels. I knocked again, a little louder, and then finally pressed the doorbell. Mrs. Elkin answered and motioned me in, then waved at Dad. I turned and waved at Dad, too, grateful that he hadn't tried to walk me to the door, because the stories would've started to fly out of his mouth, and once he started talking I never would've gotten out of there. Lauren's mom shut the door behind me.

The house smelled like Christmas, a blend of cookies and maybe a roast, but it was only the middle of September, and all that cooking was probably just her trying to keep herself busy while a basement full of freshly-minted teenagers did God-knows-what right beneath her feet. She pulled open the door and showed me into the basement, then followed me halfway down, just as she would do for every guest who arrived after me. It became the running joke of the evening, the way her feet would appear and then we knew someone else would come bounding down the steps to join us.

A boombox stationed atop a wine red card table blared *Regulate* by Warren G and Nate Dogg, and, under the dim light of a pair of red novelty bulbs, half the cheerleading squad was shaking it over by the bowls of Doritos. Beyond them, a handful of guys I didn't know (some of them with mustaches thick enough that they were visible even in that light) slouched against the wall. As soon as she noticed me, Lauren hurried over to grab the birthday card out of my hand.

"I was hoping you'd come!" she shouted over the music.

By the time I finished saying, "Happy birthday," the card was already open, and she'd pocketed the ten-dollar bill. She tossed the envelope on which I'd so carefully written her name and set the card on a pile of others. There weren't any presents so far as I could tell; everyone else must've done like me and picked a card then begged their parents for cash.

"Don't bother with the punch yet," she said, pointing to a big plastic bowl on top of a card table. "Dave should be here soon with the rest of the *ingredients*."

Lauren started to walk away, then paused, turned, and flashed a mischievous smile.

"I think someone's glad to see you." She shrugged toward the wall.

I looked in the direction she'd indicated and saw Emma, wearing a big, exaggerated grin. A small cluster of whispering, giggling girls surrounded her. I understood, then, just why I'd been invited. When Lauren first approached me in the lunch line and told me about the party, I'd taken it as a joke—after all, I couldn't recall her having ever spoken to me before. But the next day, an invitation with an address and date and starting time was dangling inside the door of my locker, stuck to the vent through which it had been slipped.

It had not crossed my mind that Emma would be there. I was just steps from the stairway at that point—I could have easily turned and run back into the kitchen, but I knew Dad was long gone, on his way home. If we'd had cell phones then, I might have manufactured a stomachache and called him back. He would have known better, but he would have chuckled into the receiver and come to get me anyway, probably played it up into a big deal when he arrived at the door. I could've used the Elkins' phone anyway, but then everyone in the room and Mrs. Elkin, in addition to Dad, would know of my fake, sudden illness. So, I was stranded. Until slightly before midnight (Dad was always early) I was stuck in a dark basement with the most notorious sexual predator in seventh grade.

I walked to the card table that held the snacks and sodas, turned my back to Emma, took a deep breath, and then poured the slowest red Solo cup of Dr. Pepper in the recorded history of mankind. I let it settle until the last bubble had popped, poured another thimble's worth, and kept this up until the thing was finally filled. Even then, I kept my back to the party and tried to look busy until Jason and Chad—two of my teammates who actually got onto the court during games—showed up and distracted everybody. They were from Lauren's side of town, the side where all the houses were brick and the license plates spelled out their drivers' names in a hodgepodge of actual letters and stand-in numbers (like 5TEVE and 8RE4NN). They'd gone home for their showers.

Emma's house was not brick. In fact, it wasn't really fastened to the ground and just kind of sat there on crooked cinder blocks. Her mom started showing up to our church a few weeks before the party, and they quickly became the congregation's pet project. There's no one Baptists love to see walk through the door more than single mothers of potentially wayward 13-year-olds. For the price of a couple delivered casseroles, a few kind glances, a well-timed shoulder pat or two, it's like a buy-one-get-one deal on salvation. Preachers know those mothers aren't going to let their little girls out of sight line; one impassioned sermon, and mom is strutting right down the powder blue aisle toward the wood-veneered altar while the music minister warbles *Just as I Am* into his lapel microphone. Once she was in the repentant fold, her daughter could go one of two ways: bite the bullet and join the flock, or live up to her full waywardness potential, get knocked up, and start the whole process over again. Either way, it was win-win for the congregation—sort of an evangelical cap and trade system.

With Emma, it started innocently enough—a wink from across the sanctuary, then a small wave or two. A note was passed (nearly intercepted by Mr. Grover): "Do you like Emma, circle yes or no." I blushed when I read it, glad to be noticed by a girl—any girl. I didn't circle anything, because I'd have been grounded for a month if my folks caught me sending notes during the sermon. I suppose she took this as playing hard to get.

Emma's mom was sick the next Sunday (a 'headache') and called to see if we had a spare seat in the car. Mom couldn't say yes fast enough. And that's when it really started to go downhill. Before Emma even had her seatbelt fastened, she had her foot hooked around my calf, and spent the whole ride running her pink jelly shoe up and down the bottom half of my leg. Her deviance completely shielded by the angles of a sub-compact, all I could do was sit there and watch my own face get redder in the rearview mirror. When we arrived, Mom pushed her seat forward and waited for me to climb out. She couldn't understand why it was taking me so long to move.

I'll say this about Emma: she was good at the game. She prayed her way right into the flock alongside her momma, but once she got out of the pew and a few paces from her mother's sight, she was something else altogether. The girl could roll just about any skirt to half its intended length. And then there was footsie under the art room table, all the way up to inner thigh while Mrs. Andrews droned on about focal lines. I'll never forgive that seating chart.

•

I'd downed one soda and had spent a good five minutes filling a second when I turned around and saw her staring and grinning from the other side of the pool table. She tugged a little at the V of her low-cut dress and arched her brows, smiled even wider. She looked like an ample-breasted she-Satan under that red light. I downed drink number two, turned back around, and repeated the whole process.

While I was doing this, I noticed in the back corner of the room a girl I'd never seen before. A light-haired girl in jeans and a sweater, leaning against the wall, alone. Through Lisa Loeb glasses, she stared at the floor, watched the heel of her right shoe kick at the stationary toe of her left. She glanced upward for a moment, and our eyes connected. I saw the smallest hint of a smile, and I swore (though because of the lighting I could never quite be certain) that she blushed just a little.

Envoys came from the far side of the pool table to tell me how glad Emma was that I'd come. That she was in love, or something to that effect. That she would not say no, should I happen to ask her out. That she had on something special under her dress. That there was a cozy spot under the stairwell where we could get to know each other *real well.* All I could ask was, "Who's the girl in the corner?"

"That's Lauren's cousin from up north," one of the girls finally told me. "Sylvia. Forget her, though. She's frigid."

I was smitten by frigid Sylvia. But I was aware no one in that room was going to *let* me be smitten by sweet, innocent, alone-in-the-corner, cleavage-covered-up Sylvia. They wanted to see me taken under that stairwell. They wanted to see me emerge flustered, winded, belt unhooked, spoiled. They wanted to see me emerge as something interesting. The part of me that had first blushed at Emma's letter wanted that, too—wanted to know what it was like to be one of the bad kids, as Ms. Jenkins said every week in Sunday school before reciting her catch phrase: "Keep 'em zipped, folks." (Despite her constant reminders, or maybe because of them, both her daughters were pregnant before junior year.) But the rest of me, the ninety-six or so percent of me that ignored the smiling girl and listened so intently to stern Sunday sermons, wished I could talk to Sylvia. And I decided, right there while I watched those carbonated bubbles pop, that I wasn't going without a fight. I slammed one more Dr. Pepper, effectively killing the two-liter (I think I drank it myself, that it had been full when I arrived). I opened the bottle of Crystal Pepsi, filled up once more, and then marched straight toward Sylvia. I was terrified. I had no idea what I would say, what I would do. But recklessly, I walked. I was about three feet from her, my mouth formed into the shape of "Hi." She looked at me nervously and, when I tried to push some sound through my vocal chords, someone grabbed my hand from behind, swung me around, and pulled me away. It was Lauren.

"Come on," she said as she tugged me across the room. "You're gonna dance with Em." She deposited me in the middle of the area rug that had become a dance floor. I stood there, my mouth hanging open, eye-to-eye with Emma. Lauren gave me one more shove from behind, right into Emma's arms. Girls giggled. A couple of guys laughed. Someone celebrated with a muffled, "Woo!" I heard someone else mumble, "Finally."

Somebody cut off poor Snoop Dogg right in the middle of his dismissal of thangs not *G* and switched discs on the boombox. So as Celine Dion explained *The Power of Love*, I had my very first slow dance. With Emma. Who kept constricting her arms around my waist, forcing me to follow her wobbly, off-rhythm sway. An entire room full of people gawked, but I couldn't stop thinking about Sylvia—how as I had approached her, she looked just as awkward as I felt. Every time I craned my neck to try and find her, Emma squeezed tighter, made sure I knew that for the next five minutes and twenty-nine seconds I was hers, and that there was nothing I could do about it. I hated how the lace from her bra jabbed into my chest. I was surprised by the tenderness with which she rested her head on my shoulder. I was embarrassed that parts of me conspicuously refused to be repulsed. After the first chorus, more couples filtered onto the carpeted space, surrounded us so that we no longer seemed to be on a stage.

Emma let go when the song ended and somebody replaced it with *Here Comes the Hotstepper*. She looked at me sweetly, expectantly. In that moment, she seemed a completely different person. She looked quiet and vulnerable. All I could think to say was: "Do you know where the bathroom is?"

She pointed to the stairs. Her face looked pained. She folded her arms across her chest and almost recoiled before turning and walking back to her friends. I stayed in the bathroom for five minutes, toweled off my face, slumped against the wall. My first dance was supposed to be with someone sweet, someone important. Not the school slut. I felt like I should pray, but had no idea how to define what I wanted to be forgiven of. Back downstairs, I leaned against one of the walls and watched everyone else mingle and laugh. I checked my watch. Only ten-thirty.

Twice more I tried to approach Sylvia. Once, Stephen stepped between us and asked me to explain where he was supposed to line up on Coach's new baseline in-bounds play. The second attempt, I made it one step past the newly fortified punch bowl when someone started the *Electric Slide*. I was jostled and nearly run over by three girls racing toward the dance floor. By the time I recovered and pointed myself back in the right direction, Sylvia was gone from her post against the wall. I turned and saw her, halfway up the stairs—on her way to the kitchen or bathroom or outside, on her way to somewhere I wasn't.

Lauren put me in Emma's arms once more, but Emma looked disappointed, held me loosely, as if she were doing this as a favor to *me*.

In the car, Dad asked how it went. When I shrugged and didn't answer, he dropped it. I knew he understood when he switched off the talk radio station and pushed my MC Hammer tape into the cassette deck. I knew how this music repulsed Dad, how he normally rolled the windows tight and relied on the A/C every time I produced that cassette from my pocket. But on that night, he left the windows down, and he even turned it up, neighbors be damned. Hammer said everything that needed to be passed between father and son. When we got home, he turned off the car, and we both sat there for what felt like ages, though it couldn't have really been more than a few minutes. Finally, he patted me on my knee.

"It'll get better, son."

He didn't mean that any more than he wanted to listen to Hammer's rhymes. But he said it anyway, and then opened his door. When I was slow to follow, he called from the door. "Come on. Get some rest."

Monday, there were stories, none of them correct. I gave up trying to fix them. Half the school thought I was a hero; the rest were split between liar and hypocrite. By Wednesday, though, the school had turned its attention to people who did actual interesting things under people's basement stairs, or who scored points during actual basketball games. There were a dozen more parties that semester. Each time I heard about one of them, I invented a new preoccupation so that I could avoid it, just in case someone happened to invite me. And when no one did, I pretended to breathe a sigh of relief.

•

I see Emma every now and then—she walks past me sometimes while I'm at work. She married a banker a few months back, and they live across town now. After the party, Sylvia went back to her home, wherever 'north' was. I never heard from her again, and Lauren just rolled her eyes the first two times I asked about her. The third time, I asked for an address and got one— one that earned me a big red *return to sender* stamp on the envelope, along with a handwritten, underlined message that said, "No such town!"

Dad's in a nursing home now—I visit every Saturday, and every Saturday he gives me a quizzical look and I explain that I'm his son. After I've had as much as I can handle (lately, it's not much) I go home to his house, where I still live alone.

I was driving home from a chat with Dad's shadow last week when I heard on the radio that Nate Dogg died. The old convenience store was leveled years ago; otherwise, I would have stopped in and bought a milkshake, poured part of it on the curb in his honor. He died of heart failure, the disc jockey said—not the way most gangsta rappers probably envision going. The station played *Regulate*, and it gave me chills—put me right back in that place, back in the middle of that dim basement. Before the song ended, my car was idling in the driveway of a house the Elkin family sold years ago.

I knocked, then rang the doorbell. Just as I was turning to walk back to my car, the deadbolt clicked, and a bald old man opened the door.

"Can I help you, son?"

"I, uh—"

I hadn't thought this through.

"I've already got a church, if that's what you're here about. And if the paperboy wants a tip—"

"That's not it," I told him. "This—this is going to sound strange. I wondered if I might, I mean—I knew the people who used to live here. Could I, maybe, take a look at your basement?"

The man scrunched his brow for a minute, looked real uneasy. He stared at my car. It was still running and I hadn't turned down the stereo. They were playing *Regulate* again.

"Just a peek," I said. "Something happened there a long time ago. It's okay if you'd rather not."

I had a tie on. I think that helped. He took a deep breath and stepped out of the doorway. "Go ahead. Nothing down there—I don't use it. I doubt you'll find what you're looking for, but good luck."

As I walked into his house, stepped once more across that foyer, I got goose bumps, and started to hope that maybe I would see or feel or remember something in that basement, something to explain that night, or explain my life, or maybe for just a moment make me feel giddy and hopeful again.

But when I reached the bottom of the stairs, I saw that he was right—it was stark empty. Even the area rug was gone. The red tint, the boom box, the card table—all long gone. But the shape of it was still the same, and I tried to picture everyone and everything in its spot, just as when I first descended those stairs. I looked at the far corner and I looked at the middle of the room where the dance floor had once been and I tried to see the two girls who had occupied those spots: one shy and sweet, the other pushy and brash. Hard as I tried to reproduce the image, I couldn't help seeing it differently this time. I saw one girl standing apart from everyone, a girl who felt out of place and just wanted to be left alone. Who probably didn't want to be there at all. Who didn't need to meet anyone. And I saw another girl, one who had been so eager to catch just an instant of my attention that she'd tried everything she knew, maybe everything she'd learned from watching her mother's own desperate flailings—a girl I hadn't bothered to talk with or listen to. I saw a father who once seemed to know everything and now couldn't tell his son from a nurse. And I felt like a very lonely man standing in an empty room, lost.

I got snapped out of it by a sound, something faint and familiar—the thumping bass, the swirling Wurlitzer piano penetrated the poured concrete wall. From my car stereo, Nate Dogg sang "The rhythm is the bass and the bass is the treble." In that moment, inside that empty space, the dumbest line in a bad song that made the strangest night of an awkward year seem oddly perfect: "The rhythm is the bass and the bass is the treble."

I thanked the old man, and he smiled at me, looked relieved I hadn't held him up at gunpoint. The radio station had gone to commercial so I put in a CD, and headed for home.

When I got there, I turned on my computer and looked up Emma's email address. Before clicking 'send,' I stared for a few minutes at the note I'd written:

Emma:
I'm sorry.

I was proud of this. It felt right. I clicked send. It was less than two minutes later when her reply came:

For what?

I didn't know whether to laugh or to be embarrassed. I didn't know whether to save or delete. But I did know that, for once, it would be right to do nothing. That this time, I should let it go.

•

I didn't notice when she walked up to the counter—I was too busy trying to make eye contact with the Auntie Anne's Pretzel girl. It's such a foreign concept, someone actually stopping at the cell phone kiosk *on purpose*. I've grown so accustomed to people walking to the far side of the mall, or darting their eyes away, acting like they're window-shopping before I can even finish saying, "Excuse me, sir, can I ask you about your cell phone plan?" And so I have no idea how long Emma stood there, watching me embarrass myself as I tried to catch the eyes of a (maybe) eighteen-year-old.

She finally coughed (one of those fake, muffled, *look-at-me* coughs), which is what caught my attention, and I jerked straight into sales mode: "Can I help you with some—oh, how are, um, how are you?"

"That's what I came by to ask *you*," she said, and I smiled at that, glad at the gesture. She had on hospital scrubs and seemed thinner, with short hair that suited her. She had glasses on with thick black rims, but there were still visible bags under her eyes.

"Oh, I'm…"

Our kiosk used to house a watch repair stand—that's the only explanation I ever came up with for why there's a vanity mirror on our counter. I caught myself glancing at it, checking to make sure my company-issued black tie was straight. She looked away while I did this, like she was window-shopping American Eagle, just the way a regular mall customer would.

"I'm good," I finally managed. She looked back at me, and her smile didn't seem quite right. Like she didn't believe me.

"How's your Dad?" she asked. "I heard he wasn't feeling well."

"That's the gentle way to put it," I said, then realized that's exactly why she'd said it that way. I probably blushed, because she looked away again and then checked her watch.

"Hey, congratulations, by the way," I told her, and she smiled, this time, for real.

"Thanks," she said.

"Sorry I couldn't make it," I lied. "I couldn't get anyone to take my shift."

"Well, we would have loved to have you there. But thanks for the present. It was so…thoughtful."

I shrugged a little and smiled. "That's what Mom always used to get everyone for weddings. She said, 'Everybody always gets toasters, but no one ever thinks of a cooler.'"

"We hadn't even thought to register for one, but you know what? We didn't have a cooler. We've used it twice already."

She shifted her weight, and I knew she'd leave soon. I saw the light flash off her ring and asked the first thing that popped into my mind, the first thing I thought might keep the conversation going, keep her there for a moment.

"How was the honeymoon?" I asked, and then my stomach sunk, because I really did not want to hear or think about the answer.

"Oh, God it was great," she said. "Aaron took me to Tuscany, where his family is from."

She waited, and I said nothing.

"Italy."

"Oh, I bet the food was amazing," I told her. "You know what I really like, is the chicken Marsala at the Olive Garden. Sometimes, I go there on payday weekends before I visit Dad, and that's what I always get. Did you have that in Italy?"

"Sure," she said, and she broke eye contact, looked at the display case full of last year's flip phone models. "Yeah, I think we did. Probably."

Then she was quiet again, and I had nothing left to ask. When she checked her watch again, I knew that I'd lost her.

"Well…" she said.

"It was good to see you, Emma."

"It was good to see you, too," she said, and she patted my shoulder, gave it a little squeeze. "You take care of yourself, okay?"

I nodded and smiled.

"Hey, you should stop by church sometime," she said. "Everyone would love to see you." I believed this, but did not want to explain how it felt to be surrounded by a room full of Dad's old friends, who couldn't bring themselves to visit him, but who played 20-questions about his health the last time I tried to sneak into the back pew. "And you've got my email address if you ever need anything."

"You know where to find me," I told her, and she waved and walked off toward the nice end of the mall, the wing with Macy's and Victoria's Secret and the covered parking deck. I like to think she'd have hugged me if it weren't for the glass display case between us.

I was pretty certain that *sales pitch* (mall slang for chatting with a lady while you're on the clock) had cost me any chance to ever get a smile from the pretzel girl. Not that I'd try to *date* a teenager, but a smile from a girl is a smile from a girl, and for 45 or so hours per week, the choices inside Oakdale Place Mall are slim. I watched Emma walk away until she disappeared, blocked from view by the kiosk where they sell oversized cookies with drawings and inscriptions done up in icing. When she was gone, I rearranged the phones and straightened all the glittery protective sleeves. I wiped down the glass cases three times. I swept for the first time in a month. I changed the light bulb that had been flickering for weeks. And when I was done with every menial task I could find, I glanced at the Auntie Anne's girl, who stopped rolling a rope of pretzel dough long enough to place her hand on her hip, roll her eyes at me, then look pointedly in the opposite direction.

•

About an hour before my shift ended, I broke my manager's number one rule and made a personal call on the clock. Nurse Mary answered and told me he was alert and ornery. "You should stop by," she told me. "This is the best day he's had in a while."

"I was planning on it. But I had a question for you. I wondered if…could I bring him a drink? I know it sounds funny, but—"

"Now you know I can't allow alcohol in here. That's just—"

"Oh, no—no, I didn't mean that. I just meant a milkshake. Vanilla. He used to really like those."

She paused. I heard her sigh.

"Well, Bess is on reception duty tonight, and you know how *she* is."

"Yeah."

"But tell you what. Don't go flashing it around when you come in, and I'll try to distract her. It's worth a try, right?"

And so I did it. I snuck two milkshakes in, held them down by my hips and walked right past the nurses' station, smiled at Mary as she pointed out something high up on the wall to distract her old battle-axe of a boss. There was a little table in his room with two seats, not dissimilar from the one at his divey convenience store, long plowed under by then for the sake of an apartment complex. Dad didn't say much of anything as I sat at that table all afternoon and into the evening. But he smiled as he drank that milkshake, and I knew, at least in spurts and fits, something inside his head was turning the proper direction. He kept trying to drink from the milkshake until far after it had slurped into oblivion. Finally, a nurse came to take the cup from him and tossed it in the trashcan by the door. I took that as my cue to leave. I reached across the bed and patted his shoulder, half expecting him to snap into dad form and offer me some advice. But it was just more quiet and I knew that was all there was left between us. On the way out, I chucked my spent cup on top of his, took a deep breath, and stepped out in the hall with the sort of finality I could only have learned from him.

five meals in paris

i

Take the last stale pastry off the hostel's tabletop buffet and pour a mug of drip coffee; recall the commandment Professor Jacobs issued a decade ago from her pulpit, the lectern of a Cuyahoga Community College literature classroom: "Everyone *must* see Paris once." Replay that moment as you sip—how her hands flailed and her brooch gleamed, how her eyes widened and her southern drawl receded every time she said it: *Paris.* The others rolled their eyes and mocked her, but you took her seriously, took as gospel that Paris was for everyone, an experience that must not be missed in a meaningful lifetime.

Forget the cab driver who last night circumnavigated the city until you owed him half the Euro notes you purchased inside the airport terminal. Forget the irritable hostel desk clerk, the snoring Finn and sexually adventurous Turks with whom you shared a dorm. Think of the gallon jug that for eight years sat like a shrine atop the apartment refrigerator, collecting every spare coin—the change from every pack of chewing gum or soda from the break room vending machine.

You nearly hid that jug, weary of sarcastic remarks from friends. But as it slowly filled you ignored more pressing uses for the cash, like last April when you let yourself fall behind a month on the electric bill rather than plunder your savings. Plane fares rose and exchange rates jackknifed but finally you rolled and counted each coin, scoured the Web for a cut-rate, off-season e-ticket from Cleveland-Hopkins. The foreman laughed so hard when you told him why you wanted a week off in February. You ignored the guys who called you Frenchie, and when someone left a beret in your locker, you smiled and wore it all day. And now, as they scrape around in coveralls, you are in *Paris.*

As you consider what waits on the other side of that weathered hostel door, remember to chew, at least a little. Sling one last sip of coffee and undertake what will become morning routine: hide securely away in your back pocket the stigma of a navy blue U.S. passport, flip coat collar upward, yank scarf tight, straighten hat, and burst out the door. Smile.

Nothing will seem common in those first moments. The stone streets are rough with charm, not from neglect like the worn asphalt back home. And the buildings—every one unique and intricate, and you'll wince just to think of the crumbling cube of concrete that holds your bed and all your belongings. Every step presents something vibrant and new—coffees and breads and roasted meats send their smells out onto the street, and the sun peeks down in strange, wonderful angles between buildings. And even though the voices around you are morning-muted, they swirl into a warm blur—remember to *breathe*.

The budget allows for one meal each day; at three in the afternoon, split the difference between mealtimes and smile at the providence of bold letters on a street cart, a word that springs back from the mind's recesses, a remnant of high school French class, *boulangerie*. Try to read panini descriptions in French, but when impatience takes over, switch to parenthesized English. Near the bottom of the clapboard, find a safe selection—bread with five cheeses, and it's even simple to order in French: "Un sandwich avec cinq fromages, s'il vous plait."

"Comin' right up," the man behind the counter will say in a manufactured drawl, grinning in acknowledgment of both the effort and the hacksaw you've taken to his native language.

Do not hand him the money while ordering, as you would back home—he won't take it. First, watch him pull the sandwich from the display case and clamp it with a heated press. Only after the man has wrapped and handed you the bread/cheese torpedo will he accept your coins. Trade 'merci' formalities with him, but don't bother with beaucoup—no one ever really says that in France. Pull back the paper wrapping, and keep the bites slow:

this has to last until breakfast. Burn to memory the mild crunch of that first bite—just bread—and then the second when the cheeses get involved, their flavors alternating sharp and mild, strong and smooth.

Between bites, scan the streetscape for the housewives carrying armloads of fresh bread, the boisterous vendors, the plucky artists, the hopscotching children whose photographs illustrated *Introduction à Francais*. Whose images distracted you, those nights in an attic bedroom atop your parents' row house, when you should've been studying the *language* of France, rather than the daydream of *Away*. The Cuyahoga was on fire back then; above glowing pilot lights, the sky alternated between grey and black—never clear. *Away* was a beautiful idea. Today, finally, *Away* is a beautiful place, even if you see none of the people your textbook promised.

Take a final bite of the sandwich as you stroll brick-inlaid Rue Mouffetard, teeth grinding in slow circles—victims of that sad mechanism, restraint. When the panini is gone, wait awhile before chasing its remnants with still water from a grocery store, just like your dog-eared second-hand guidebook recommends.

That evening, tease the budget and sip espresso at a table in the front window of Le Café de Flore. When a waiter in vest and bow tie offers a small tin pitcher of milk, nod. This is a matter of volume, not taste—it will double the size of your drink, double the number of sips, double the length of your lease on the seat. Marvel at erratic taxicabs and gaudy winter clothes as everyone floats by in a blur. Buy a second thimble-sized coffee shot to further delay the walk home.

ii

Dump sugar and packets of processed creamer into the hostel's burnt coffee. Drink it fast, and no one will notice it's blonder than Marilyn. Pour a forbidden refill when the breakfast man looks away, distracted by the washing of trays.

Walk all morning, walk to weariness, smile, look up—always upward, at the balconies, the verandas, the gold foiling, at the intricate bronze work of statues memorializing people you'll never hear of or care about. Don't look down—the beauty of Paris is upward, even if the sky is charcoal.

In the afternoon, it's another street vendor—this time for a *crêpe*. After ordering, watch the cook eat a bite of something, then lick his fingers one at a time. Without so much as wiping on a rag, he'll pour your batter over a circular form, spread it thin, wait for the heat to do its work, flip, fill, top, wrap then thrust your food forward, smile, and say "voila." Ignore those unclean fingers and accept it, crush between your molars the sweet concoction of batter and sugar crystals. Smile. It's Paris—*smile*. With hints of *crêpe* lingering on your palate, walk by the Tour d'Eiffel and Arc de Triomphe, see their grand forms and magnificent arches from the ground, but don't pay to climb any stairs. Paris offers plenty of those for free. Later, shell out ten Euro to enter the Lourve because, well, you *must*. Once inside, follow the thick evening crowds to the right, see Venus and Mona, then peel away to the museum's left bank, to the lonely rooms of paintings no one has in mind as they're patted down by guards looking for bombs and spray paint. Marvel at the splendor and sadness in the ancient shades before you. Note that the painted forms are your only neighbors. Inside this famous building in this bustling city, you are *alone*.

At night, duck into a bar, someplace cramped and dim. Buy the biggest, cheapest drink they've got and watch students carry animated but whispered arguments. Imagine they're discussing something profound or sexy. Sip and sip, watch and listen and long until your glass is empty. Return to the hostel, slip quietly into the room, trying not to wake anyone until you realize there's no one else—you're the first one to return. Pull the sheets up to your chin and fall asleep before the Turks can stumble back in and keep you awake all night.

iii

Same god-awful breakfast, but it's still free. Swipe an extra croissant (the last one) and slather it in strawberry jam, because cheap croissants in Paris are just as dry as cheap croissants in Ohio. Paris by foot will begin to take its toll. As the day unravels, muscles will resist footsteps first with a dull ache, then with the hint of a blister on the smallest right toe. Rest by taking a seated meal amongst chatty students at a café along Rue Sorbonne, one where the wooden patio chairs all face the street. The front row will be filled, but the second row is not so bad, and so it's *petit dejeuner pour un*, but the waitress will roll her eyes and say "that means breakfast, not little lunch." Study the English menu she'll produce from the right pocket of her apron. Angle it away from others so no one can see the conspicuous absence of accents aigu or grave.

When the waitress finally returns engulfed in the scent of a prolonged smoke break, order the special, a small salad, followed by chicken encrusted with something that has no precise English translation and so its title has been left in French. But the picture looks nice, so that's where you will point, and it'll be tea and tap water. She will bring Perrier and will not understand—or pretend not to—when you explain you want water from the sink or basin or pipe, and she'll summon another waitress and make a scene. Voices will escalate, arms will flail, people with English and French menus will stare—just take the damn Perrier, count it as sunk cost.

When the food arrives, ignore the pulsing blister on your toe, ignore the seeping blood that will have to be bleached from your white sock—focus instead on the flavors, the encrusting which turns out to be some sort of spiced cheese. Don't take it personally when the tea never arrives except on the bill, or when you notice the unwanted Perrier cost six Euro. Just pay the bill and go. Brush aside what loud curses follow you onto the sidewalk when the waitress discovers a fifty-cent tip, despite assurances by both the menu and your guidebook that tips are unnecessary. Walk quickly, and think only of the food, which rests heavy in a satisfied stomach.

Eveningtime, explore the mad colors, jagged shadows, manic sounds of Saint Michel's tightly drawn streets. Walk with confident purpose past restaurateurs who shout at you in English, "Couscous!" When one of them grabs your arm, draw back. He will point to a photo menu taped to the window. With bulging eyes and aggressive posture he will persist: "Couscous! For you, drink included!" You'll understand by then how dearly an included drink can cost. When he tightens his grip, shout: "No! No couscous!" He will release you. As you exit the narrow street, Notre Dame will stand stark and backlit before you, will steal your breath. Fall in love with this place, with this moment; forgive those who would try to tarnish its beauty.

iv

Explore further reaches of the city, legging it out to avoid Metro fares. Window shop stores in which you'd never be welcome—black-clad doormen will glare and fold their arms to make this quite clear. From the steps of Sacre Coeur, use Notre Dame, the Pantheon, a bent black ribbon of the Seine to estimate the hostel's location. Feel at first elated about how far you've come—then crushed at how many roofs, how much distance separates you from your goal. The sun will set and street signs won't match the names printed on your hostel-issued mess of a wrinkled map—go ahead and say it out loud: *lost*. No one will respond to your feeble 'excusez moi' and either there are a dozen Chinese dry cleaners in this neighborhood—each with an inexplicable stuffed duck hanging upside-down in the window— or you're walking circles down a street the map proclaims straight. Forestall worry by focusing on your toe, which throbs its way to the front of your mind, precludes even the instinct to panic. Try the Metro, but its ticket machine will be out of order—they always are. The steps back to street level will seem the embodiment of defeat.

Desperately hungry, pull the bill of your cap low over embarrassed eyes when entering McDonald's to order a value meal by holding up three fingers. Astonishingly, this will tax the interpretive skill of four employees. As you sit alone in the molded plastic booth and drag soggy French fries through two packets of ketchup that cost a Euro each, conversations and lovely accents will fill the restaurant. Grimace as you realize *this* is the place where you'll encounter the most actual Parisians living their actual lives.

v

Twist a faded black necktie around a white collar, giving the knot dimples in the mirror. Run through your hair a dab of gel from the corner sundry. Run across your cheek the 4-Euro single-blade Bic, lubricated by hostel soap. Jacket on, shoes shined with a square of sink-dampened toilet paper—it's okay to smile at the makeshift job you've done in putting yourself together. In keeping yourself together.

Tablecloths will be sharp white, the array of silverware will dazzle and perplex. Waiters will maneuver with immaculate strides and precise, angular gestures. Blacks and whites, silvers and golds, boisterous laughs—this night will embody the Paris you expected, will embody hope, escape, *Away*. Wave off the English version and order from the set menu in broken but admirable French.

The wine will be deep red and heavy, will race quickly through your veins, will numb your toe, your worn muscles, your tired mind. Take another sip, then slow yourself. Savor each bite of the light, flaky bread, ignoring the thought that it's just bread, nothing substantively different than the loaf you could have bought at the 24-hour Kroger two blocks from home.

The soup will be creamy and flavorful, but don't linger over it so long that the waiter wordlessly swipes a half-full bowl when he brings the fish course. Though you haven't touched a speck of seafood since third grade (when you vomited cafeteria fish sticks and chocolate milk all over the fold-out lunch table) push aside leafy garnish and fork the tender fibers of filet. Check to see if anybody is looking before dousing it with a squeeze of the lemon that is almost certainly ornamental. Chew quickly so that the bits of flesh do not have a chance to stick on the caps of your molars or slip into the chasm between gum and cheek. Chase each bite with wine.

The main dish will arrive drizzled in a deep brown sauce and surrounded by a small forest of inedible greenery. But as the knife slides along the entrée's edge, the meat will be grey and tough. You will want to push it away, but years of your grandmother's 'clean-your-plate' commands have become intrinsic, and so you will continue, repressing the urge to let your mind freely think what you know it wants to: that in this moment of *fulfillment*, what you really want is a greasy burger with a refillable paper bucket of soda and cubed ice. Concentrate instead on the slim flickering candle that lights your table, on the waiter's finely groomed mustache—on anything that makes Paris feel like it's supposed to.

The cheese plate will arrive, a sweet respite. Each bite will be lustrous, but your stomach will feel bloated by the foods that already reside there. Then, the dessert—cheesecake (more cheese!). Quietly wrestle down the entire beige triangle.

The dark coffee will appear majestic and expensive when it arrives in the white porcelain mug atop a saucer. But sip after sip, it tastes just like the instant stuff you make each morning. This disappointment, you will decide, is a welcomed one.

When the check comes, place the colorful bills into the thin leather portfolio without pausing to calculate or convert. Walk out the door and catch a glimpse of a raven-haired Parisienne, ruby-lipped and sucking on a cigarette, complete with a black turtleneck. Smile at this cinematic perfection until she speaks—in a British accent.

Just a short walk back to bed, but you will weave and bob—delay. Relish the chance to pull this air once more through your lungs, to see Paris through the lens of your own retina. Begin, already, to filter your memory, to shape the stories you will tell coworkers and friends and family of the wonders you've seen and felt and tasted. Decide which memories to leave behind. Plan the argument you will use to prove the professor right, to prove yourself right, that Paris *must* be seen, that there is nothing like it. That yours is a meaningful lifetime. Check your watch.

The cab will take you directly to the airport this time, sparing money but robbing you of one final ride amongst the monuments, the grand buildings. Watch the empty 5 a.m. sidewalks, the streetlamps, the quiet homes blur past. Outside the heart of the city, the suburbs look like they could be the suburbs of anyplace. They look like they could be the suburbs of home.

Across the lap of a sleeping businessman in the window seat, watch the daybreak departure through that thin oval film of glass as the plane curls up and away, leaving beneath you the city of flickering lights, a city that from the separation of a couple of moments and a few thousand feet carries an amber glow strikingly similar to the hue of the streetlamp canopy that on Monday will guide your way to third shift at the plant.

waiting out the apocalypse

On one side of the river, a troubled old town waited, its levees about to be topped. On the other, farmers vacated land that would be flooded by the explosives John Abrams' tug pushed upstream. One way or another, people's lives were about to be ruined—which was something Abrams found himself repeatedly pushing out of his mind. In twenty-three years steering barges up and down the Mississippi, he'd seen it swell and churn under the pressure of ceaseless rains, and he'd seen it shrink up anemic and thin under the scorching July sun. But he'd never had the power to shape its direction. It was one thing to push beans or fuel oil. Things that fed people, that put them to work. This task was something altogether new to him. His hand tightened against the wheel.

He tried his best to ignore the spotlights that flanked his vessel and to keep his focus on the high, churning water before him, steering with the same calm demeanor with which he'd carried a thousand loads of coal toward Minneapolis or grain toward New Orleans. As his barge pulled out of the bend at New Madrid, he reached toward the tug's throttle. He hesitated for a moment, then picked up his copy of the orders, the word *URGENT* stamped in the margin with bright red ink. He read the document once more—as if he hadn't already memorized it—and then steadied his rudder for the final straight approach, kicked the propellers to full. Captain Abrams felt his boat and its cargo thrust forward. He radioed his adjustments to the Coast Guard vessels, then looked to his right, where a stern-faced Coast Guard captain waved acknowledgement from his lit-up pilothouse before bumping up the speed of his own cruiser.

•

Under the clapboard awning of his porch in Cairo, Illinois, Ezekiel Smith wrapped an arm tight around his daughter, Jade. Piled around them were their movable possessions, stuffed and duct taped into two-dozen cardboard boxes. Ezekiel tapped the *Enter* key on his cell phone to make sure it was still working, to make certain he hadn't missed the call. One sliver of a battery icon still showed. The phone would go dead any moment, and Ezekiel would have to decide: keep waiting for James and his pickup to arrive or leave everything behind and make for the floodgate by foot. He dialed once more, listened to the phone ring until he heard his brother's voicemail greeting. Ezekiel hung up and held his hand out from under the awning. The rain was falling harder. *How the hell could any water be left up there?* he wondered. *And why did the Lord see fit to send it all down in this one spot?* Ezekiel turned to his right, looked at the levee that rose from the nub of his dead-end street. Up top, dozens of A-shirted guardsmen rushed to stack sandbags (he'd tried to join them days ago—wanted to help somehow—but was shooed off by a stern officer who said someone untrained would just be in the way). As the bags flew into place, Ezekiel swore he saw splashes of the Mississippi flying up into the sky; he prayed that they were just flecks of loose sand.

He checked his watch, nervous, and then told his daughter over and over again in a low voice what he very much hoped to be true: "It's going be all right, Jade. It's going to be okay."

•

In Birds Point, Missouri, Franklin Wilks listened to the rain drum down on the slate roof above his porch. He sat on the cold surface fashioned from fieldstones his grandfather had collected by hand. His back rested against blood-red bricks of a home built by the same man in the same fashion. Franklin watched even more rain fall into a chain of small ponds that had formed where corn stalks should've already been waist-high. Instead, he saw the swollen carcasses of seeds as they bobbed on the surface, long drowned, yet still floating. For weeks on end, it had dripped and poured, sprayed and pounded. And now Franklin sat alone on the stone floor because he'd sent his wife and son away two days earlier, along with a rental truck full of their belongings— including the hand-made porch rocker he'd normally have occupied. He had waved at them as they started down the driveway. Almost, he had laughed. Almost, at the sight of his wife Janie and the twins, Bonnie (the dog), and Frank (the blue-ribbon 4H goat) squeezed into that truck cab. It had almost been sad enough to be funny.

The battery powered CB in Franklin's lap crackled and beeped then squawked warnings from a neighbor: down the road, maybe just a mile away by now, Missouri National Guard MPs were on their way with signed orders and loaded guns, ready to escort him off the land. Ready to move him off what he called home, and what they called a floodway. "You're the last hold-out," the voice on the CB said. "Good luck. Don't get yourself hurt."

Franklin reached into his shirt pocket for a bag of sunflower seeds and popped a handful into his mouth. It wasn't so much that he wanted to eat the seeds, more that he wanted something to spit. To keep his blood cool. He dug his heels against the floorboards and waited, determined to hold onto his plot of earth until forced off.

●

On the shoulder of Interstate-57, James Smith pulled a jack and a dummy tire from behind the passenger seat. As he kicked the wrench and threw his full weight into budging a rusted bolt, he saw a convoy of troop transports speeding southbound, escorted by a state patrol cruiser that hugged the white line. James stood and pressed himself against the side of his truck to avoid getting hit by the cop, turned his face away from the whipping wind until the trucks passed. He watched them drive off in the direction he ought to be going—fresh-faced soldiers laughing and cutting up, calm as can be inside those trucks. This relief mission was fresh air for them, he knew—it was relaxing, a break from monotony, from drills, from their workweeks. Fill some sandbags, stand guard, boss some folks around, eat some different food, camp out a few nights, then go home. Hell of a lot better of an assignment than a tour in the desert—James understood that much from his own experience. But for his brother and niece, this was life and death. *He'd* have no police escort; no Good Samaritan was going to stop and quicken his repairs. Those troops wouldn't have been flying by so fast if water weren't about to spill through—or maybe this batch hadn't been called for sandbagging at all—but to enforce the evacuation. To clear the town before the levees topped. James kicked once more at the wrench, and finally dislodged the first lug nut. He pulled his cell phone from his pocket. No signal. He bent down to reset the wrench and start in on the second nut.

Crazy man, James thought as he kicked the second lug loose enough to be finished off by hand. *If he'd have moved north with the rest of the family, we'd be having a beer right now, watching this mess on TV.*

•

When Franklin saw the top of a green jeep driving down the levee access road, he stood slowly, stretched, and walked through the front door into the nearly empty living room. He picked up an old twelve-gauge and carried it back to the porch. It wasn't loaded—Franklin had never used it on anything bigger than a duck, and had no intention of doing so. But he thought it would make a fine accessory—something to make the MPs sweat a little. They *ought* to sweat a little, he figured, when forcing someone off land bought fair and square. Franklin had nothing against the soldiers, figured they'd probably be kids. His problem was with the people who wrote the orders. He'd make *them* sweat, if he could. But he wasn't likely to run across the order writers so he settled back onto the porch floor, shifted around so that his cricked back was in the least painful position he could manage. He stretched out his legs, laid the gun across his lap so it'd be visible from the driveway. The Jeep was close enough now that it looked like a real thing, not an olive-drab speck, but a vehicle with windows and tires and a driver inside.

•

Mayor Giles tried to organize his cluttered desk while the newsmen focused their cameras and adjusted their portable spotlights. When the reporters started with their questions, the mayor, (who wore a fleece sweatshirt with the high school's Pilot logo on it and a plain red baseball cap) stared into a camera and answered as calmly as he could.

"I think it's selfish, and it's sad," he said, when asked about Missouri Governor Johnson's assertion that Cairo should be flooded to save cropland in his state. "Beans over people? You've got to be out of your mind."

"But all the people would be evacuated first," a reporter said.

"It's just following the plan," Mayor Giles said. "It's what engineers designed this system for. Those folks over in Missouri, they're hard workers and good folks, and I don't wish this on anyone. But they bought land for pennies on the dollar because it's a federal flood plain, designed to spare this city and others, all up and down the river. The land should be put to its intended purpose, and that's all I've got to say." A roomful of reporters waved their notebooks and shouted over each other, asked questions about crop values and soil erosion and pollution. When his forced smile had outstayed its welcome, he breathed deeply and stared right into a camera lens, then said, "Listen, folks—it sounds like it's a scientist you want to talk to. All I know is people, and I've got a city full of them, poor ones, mostly, and they're waiting for the help they've been promised by law. If it doesn't come, they're going to lose what little they've got on this Earth. That's what I know, and that's the only answer I've got left to give. We're sitting here, waiting for an—an apocalypse to come over those walls, and that's got no business being allowed to happen." A newspaperman from St. Louis tried to ask one more question, but Mayor Giles gave him a look that said shop was closed, and the camera operators switched off their lights and started to pack their gear.

The mayor sat back in his chair for a moment, used his sleeve to wipe sweat from his forehead, then opened his desk drawer and pulled out a pair of hefty cotton work gloves. When the last reporter had cleared from his office, he switched off the overhead light, locked the door, and started back toward the sandbag line.

•

"I had a flat," James said over the phone, soon as he got a signal. Ezekiel fought off the urge to curse—at this juncture, his daughter didn't need to hear anything but sweetness. Ezekiel took a deep breath and asked, "How long you set back?" How long's it going to be?"

"I just got moving again, and I'm a good three hours away, I suppose."

"That's not so bad," Ezekiel said, mostly for his own benefit.

"I'm not sure the spare's going to make it, though. I'll have to stop off and check on a replacement."

"I'll tell you, James, *I* can wait. Not sure the water will, though."

James was quiet for a minute, and through the phone Ezekiel heard a tractor-trailer roar by.

"You get real nervous," James said, "I'd say put your things up in the attic and meet me outside the gate."

"That might be the thing," Ezekiel said. "I'll call and let you know." With the Mississippi River bridge to Missouri and the Ohio River bridge to Kentucky already shut, there was only one exit left—a tunnel under the city's rear floodwall. If that shut, there would be no leaving, and there would be no returning to retrieve belongings—until it was all over.

"You wanna go for a walk, honey?" he asked Jade.

She nodded and stood.

Ezekiel dug an umbrella from one of the boxes. He held it with one hand, and took his daughter's little palm with the other and they walked toward the seawall to take one more look at just how hard the river was pushing.

As they walked through a downtown largely abandoned decades earlier—at no fault of the water—Ezekiel noticed water streaming down the damp pavement of Ohio Street. It started as a trickle, like the runoff from someone watering a lawn. Within a few minutes, the water covered the toes of his work boots, flowing from the confluence point, the southwestern tip of town where the Ohio and Mississippi had risen together to form a vast, gurgling lake. *Lake Katrina*, Ezekiel heard men call it the night before at Mack's Diner. This didn't amuse him as it had the others, how they'd howled and cackled at that remark. As they walked, Ezekiel thought of his brother stuck along the highway, about himself and his daughter stuck inside a sunken island of a town. Everyone stuck, everyone waiting. He couldn't think of *anything* that might make him howl like those men had.

Ezekiel led Jade to a high point along the wall, a solid concrete segment, and helped her up top. Upstream, a couple of the sandbaggers waved to Ezekiel.

When they were all the way at the top, Jade gasped at all the water in front of her. She stood sideways, the conjoined rivers on one side and the town on the other, and Ezekiel watched her eyes bounce back and forth between the solid ground, which seemed so far below, and the water, which seemed to close. Then she looked out at the choppy water and asked, "Is this what an ocean looks like, Daddy?"

"Oceans are bigger than this. But not so mean."

He wrapped an arm firmly around her and made sure she was secure. He reached his foot over the edge, tapped the toe of his boot into the deep brown water. Below the wall, there should have been a park, green grass, a monument at the confluence point, steel and concrete in the shape of a steamboat hull—the river should have been a good hundred yards away. And there he was, touching it with his boot sole.

"Is that a tree, Daddy?"

Jade pointed out into the water, where a full sycamore—roots, limbs, green leaves and all—bobbed up and down, sucked under by the current and then shoved back up.

"Sure is, sweetheart. Let's get back home."

•

About fifty workers waited along the levee as Captain Abrams steered toward the bank. Soldiers with shouldered machine guns kept watch over the demolition site. Bold floodlights illuminated workers who bustled atop the wall and the shoreline along which the Captain was to anchor. Shore-bound men with orange-glowing batons directed him toward the mooring point, guiding him as a landing crew would a jumbo jet. If he hadn't been white-knuckled from the mission, Captain Abrams might have enjoyed the star treatment. As it was, he simply followed the batons, eager to dock his cargo and haul as fast upstream—away from the blowout area—as he could before the torch was lit. Gently, he manipulated the thrust and angle of the barge, massaged it into place. Twenty yards from shore, he let off the steering lever long enough to press the docking siren—even though he knew his seasoned crew would already be waiting in the correct spots, ready to tie down and secure the load.

•

Lieutenant Amy Brown pulled up to the drive of an old brick farmhouse. As soon as she saw the shotgun draped over the resident's lap, she picked up her radio receiver.

"I got a live one here," she said. "Anybody nearby, I could use an assist."

No one answered, so she checked her address list, checked her pistol, and got out of the jeep.

"Mister Wilks," she called in the friendliest voice she could muster toward someone with a gun on his lap. She waved to emphasize the kindness; the man on the porch gave a half-nod, then spat off the porch into a hedge.

"Mister Wilks, she repeated as she approached the porch. "Lieutenant Amy Brown, Missouri National Guard, forty-second MP Unit. Sir, I'm sorry to inform you I've got an evacuation order."

"You're sorry…to *inform* me?"

"Yes, sir, very sorry. But I must inform you. And I must ask you to set aside the firearm. I'm not the enemy."

"If you're not the enemy," Franklin said, "who the hell is?"

He stood slowly, then set the gun against his house.

She watched with cool focus, ignored the impulse to move her hand toward the weapon at her hip. *Calm*, she thought. *Calm.*

"I'll ask it again," he said. "Then who is?"

"Well," she said, "I suppose the water."

"Then you're proposing I shoot at the water? Because it sounds to me like the Army Corps prefers to aim its firepower at the levee. Maybe that's the enemy, then?"

"Sir, I know this is hard, but—"

"You know this is hard? My family's farmed this land since 1894. And you're going to give my house a bath. You're going to blow out a perfectly good levee to send soot and chemicals and god-knows-what-else onto my farmland to save a run-down town most people wouldn't drive through if their life depended on it. Maybe let me do the same to you, then I'll listen while you tell me just how hard this all is."

"You live on a federal floodplain, sir." She stepped forward onto the one brick stair between the ground and his porch. She watched him for a reaction, but saw nothing new. Just cold eyes and resolve. "I'm just following my orders."

"You're following some stupid orders, then," he said. "Sacrifice my livelihood to save a city that keeps suffocating itself? Doesn't sound like an order worth following."

Franklin Wilks stepped forward and folded his arms. Behind the drape of clouds, the sun was setting. He pointed toward the river, and for the first time since arriving, she took her eyes off him, and followed his boney finger. Upriver maybe a mile, a halo of artificial light cut into the dim of twilight. "So that's it?" he asked, pointing. "That's the spot?"

"That's the floodway breach," she said. "They're preparing it right now. The barge is in place, and they're pumping explosives into the ground. Mister Wilks, please..." She stepped forward, both boots firmly on the porch. "We've got to go now. It's not safe. I can give you a moment to gather your things. Everyone else has evacuated—including your family, according to my paperwork."

"So it's just me," he said.

"Yes, sir."

"I suppose you have to escort me? Like a prisoner, right off my own property."

She nodded, then glanced over her shoulder toward the lights. "Please be quick, sir."

He nodded and turned around, then walked into his home, shut the door. Lieutenant Smith heard the deadbolt click. "Son of a—" she said, quiet but harsh. She heard him chuckling on the other side of the door.

•

On the way home, Ezekiel noticed a group of men congregated in Douglass Park. He took a two-block detour, despite Jade tugging on his arm. "*That's* not the way home," she said, but he told her it was okay—that he just needed to see something. *Something* turned out to be men piling sandbags around half the park's sun-bleached asphalt basketball court. The workers were joined by half a dozen reporters and cameramen with headsets and laminated credential badges. As a reflex, Ezekiel sneered at out-of-towners who swooped in for a good picture of misery. *They're everywhere*, he thought. He shook his head and tried to ignore them.

"What's going on?" he asked, as soon as he got within earshot.

Ed Jackson looked up and waved, stuck the blade of his shovel firmly into the sand pile, then approached Ezekiel and Jade.

"How's my girl?" he asked, and knelt down for a hug. Jade smiled from ear-to-ear before she wrapped her arms around him and said "Good."

Ed was a tall man, thin and stringy, just like he'd been when he and Ezekiel played varsity basketball and baseball together. Ed was about the last of Ezekiel's close school buddies left in town. Most had taken off about as quick as (or even before) they'd had diplomas in hand—off to Chicago or St. Louis, even Paducah—anyplace that wasn't Cairo. Even in the muck Ed wore black slacks and a white button-down with the sleeves rolled up to the elbows. Ezekiel couldn't remember the last time he'd seen his friend without a necktie. Three months earlier, Ed had baptized Jade—had cradled her head in his palm and lowered her into a far calmer version of the same Mississippi that was about to bust through the floodwalls. On that day, when the songs had been sung, when the participants' clothes had sun-dried and the picnic had finished, Ed had forsaken their normal, firm handshake. Instead, he'd hugged Ezekiel, and he'd held on so tight with those stringy arms. When he finally let go, he flicked what looked like the start of a tear from his left eye.

"It's amazing," Ed had said, "The calm of children. I baptize a grown man, and he's tense as can be, scared to death I'm going to let him drift off to the Gulf. Your Jade, though—calm as can be. I wish I had that kind of peace about me."

Against the backdrop of clinking shovels and clicking camera shutters, the minister reached out for Ezekiel's shoulder and squeezed it hard, and again held the little girl up as an example.

"She's right, you know. Long as we're alive and we've got the Lord, there's nothing to be but *good*."

"Easy for her to say," Ezekiel said.

Ed looked left and right, turned toward the men behind them.

"All this," he said, "This is home. But this isn't a promised land. Just a place to stay. Leaving won't kill us, you know, when the time comes."

"Well, that time better hold out a while. If James doesn't get his rickety truck down here fast enough, we'll have nothing left but our shirts."

"Will we have pants?" Jade asked.

"And pants," Ezekiel said. He patted Jade on the top of her head and the two men smiled.

"Could be worse," Ed said. "Not sure how, but things could be worse. You can't go renaming yourself Job just yet."

"So what is all this?" Ezekiel asked. "Shouldn't the bags be over there?" He pointed toward the levee. Ed shook his head, folded his arms across his chest. "Good Lord is giving us a real solid hint, I think. It's not enough the water's coming over the wall. Now it's pushing up underneath. Here, look."

Ezekiel had to stand on a cinder block to see over the wall of sandbags—half of the basketball court was gone, evaporated into a sinkhole—a giant boil of soupy sand and sediment. Water was churning up through the middle of the slurry, a brand new pond gurgling and pushing through, rising fast.

Ezekiel lifted Jade so she could see. "How'd the water get *there*?" she asked.

He just shook his head.

"Mayor's heading up here to take a look. As soon as he sees this, he's going to evacuate. Take your girl and get out now, Zeke. I mean it. Forget your blasted *things* and move."

"But James isn't—"

"Lord gave you feet," Ed said. "It's about time to use them."

He took one more look at the sandbaggers, how they moved furiously, wildly, in the face of a cause even their leader was calling lost. These were men he'd grown up with, had gone to school with, worshipped with. Men whose mothers babysat him and whose fathers paddled him for acting up in Sunday school. And when he had left Jade with a babysitter two days earlier, intent on helping, these men had sent him off even faster than the soldiers had. "Go take care of your kid," Ed had said, his head shaking a resolute *no*. There were other fathers working on the walls, working the bag lines, but their kids were either older, or had a living mother. Ezekiel hated it—he felt useless—but he understood. It was three days after the sandbagging started that he finally resigned to call James and ask for a ride out. "You've really got to get yourself a car, cousin," James had said. Then he followed with, "Oh, hell—of course I'll come get you. I'll take off in the morning."

Ezekiel wished he had those days back, and even hours. He lingered just a few seconds longer, watched the shovels and sand fly, watched the water rise even quicker. *Hopeless*, he thought, and then he looked up around at the crumbling town. *Hopeless*.

Another worker, Edward Albee, caught Ezekiel's eye and shot a harsh look, then pointed away from the sinkhole.

"Get her out of here, you crazy bastard."

Jade giggled and asked, "What's a bastard?"

"It's somebody that loves his daughter very much. Come on, let's go."

He picked Jade up so they could move faster.

•

Franklin Wilks sat with his back against the front door. His head and shoulders slumped. He ran a finger across smooth floorboards he'd spent his life crossing. How much water would cover this spot? How much silt? He imagined fish swimming around in his living room—if the house could even hold up when that first wave surged through the breach. Most likely, he knew, every last brick of the place would wash away. Fish in the living room might be the *best* possibility.

He knew sacrifice was a virtue—he'd heard plenty of ministers and politicians say that, and he mostly believed them. He knew he'd been fortunate that the floodway had been left unused this long. He wouldn't mind, he thought, if the river came over on its own. If he'd been allowed to stack bags, side-by-side with his neighbors and friends, to work at saving his property the same way folks across the river could. But for someone to flip a switch and inundate his life—that was too much. The skin of his back sensed the vibration of every rap against his door. The scolding sound of the woman's voice calling his name made him sick to the gut—the only people with any business taking that tone with him were his parents and— maybe—his wife. Not his pastor, not his boss, and certainly not some twenty-year-old with boots and a glorified pop gun. He would not follow this woman off his own land. He would not go this way. It was too much. He said it out loud: "Too much!" He refused to listen to the MP's response, and instead slammed his fist against the floor once, twice, a third time, until the heel of his right hand was throbbing and red. He stood and climbed up the shrugging old stairway, two steps at a time so he didn't have to hear the miserable groan of every board. He opened his bedroom window and stuck his head out. Blocked by an eave, he couldn't see the shouting soldier below. But in the distance, he saw the silhouette of a barge amongst all those bright lights. He strained his ears, tried to make out voices. He knew better— there was no way sound would carry that far. But he could imagine them counting slowly, loudly, annoyed—just like his sisters had years ago during hide-and-seek. Here he was again— hiding one more time, waiting out the countdown quiet, still, alone. He climbed out that window, scaled his slick slate roof and sat right down on its apex. The best hiding place on the whole wide-open property.

•

Mayor Giles tried to prepare himself as he approached the sinkhole. He had grown used to work crews and sandbags, the tinny sound of shovels sliding into sand piles, the deep barks of foremen shouting instructions. Those parts he could handle. Those parts made him proud of his town, of Cairo's *people*. Ed Jackson reached out his big, calloused hand, and helped the mayor up to the top of the bags, a good twelve feet high.

"Holy God," the mayor said. "Holy God."

The mayor felt Ed's hand clamp down on his shoulder and he was glad—half for the steadying aid, half for the comfort.

"There's no stopping it," Mayor Giles said. "No stopping it, is there?"

No one answered, and he stood, watched the water bubble in the center of the basketball court, watched the level rise. He clinched his eyes shut, then took a deep breath and climbed down the sandbag wall. As he walked away, he heard the sounds of work fall quiet. He'd never heard his town this silent—no car tires, no barge horns, no voices. Even the birds seemed to have fled, leaving just the tiny taps of more rain.

He looked up at the sky, but with all those thick clouds blocking the way, he didn't bother asking God for mercy or help. He was alone. The mayor turned around to the men. "You've done good work here, as good as anyone could've done. Go get your families and your belongings. It's time to go."

One-by-one, the men climbed down and dispersed toward their homes. The mayor lingered until the last of them had gone. He pulled a wireless radio from his pocket, called back to city hall.

"Blast the siren," he said. "Check the lists of who's still in town and go door-to-door—make sure no one gets left behind."

He stood there alone, surveyed his hollow town. Not five minutes after the workers dispersed, their mayor stood alone and watched water from the sinkhole destroy the manmade barrier. It splashed onto the remainder of the basketball court before dispersing and turning the entire park into a shallow lake. As he turned toward city hall, the siren blared its first warning. His arms grew goose bumps at that awful noise. He wondered if he'd ever again see any of these streets intact, or any of these buildings. He wondered if, in a day's time, any of it would still stand, whether there would be anything for residents—for him—to come home to.

•

Ezekiel and Jade had just reached their doorstep when the last siren went off—the fifteen-minute warning. The gate was coming down.

"Stay here," Ezekiel said. "Don't move." He gave Jade his best *I mean business* look until she nodded.

He ran inside and picked up two suitcases. No time to take the boxes upstairs, or even back inside. He bolted back outside with the luggage. "It's time to run, honey."

They ran through the rain with no umbrella this time. Cars zipped by—the last few left in town—their tires rattling against deep potholes, sloshing around water that covered the roadbeds. Jade giggled and hopped in the deepening water. Ezekiel wanted to stop her, to tell her how very serious this all was, but he couldn't bring himself to do it.

"Faster, Jade," was all he could manage.

•

He did not move when he heard the hinges breaking on the front door, or when he heard the stairs groaning inside. Franklin Wilks watched the last remnants of daylight dissipate over his family's land. He imagined the landscape covered by ten, twenty, maybe thirty feet, of water, treetops and silo domes peeking out above the current. He clenched his eyes and listened to the soldier, who stepped through the window gable and joined him on the roof.

"Mister Wilks, it's time—one way or another."

"Put that away," he said. He opened his eyes and saw that he'd guessed right, that her right hand was clutching the butt of her handgun, that her finger was slightly trembling inside the trigger guard.

He dropped his head, said, "I'll come now."

The woman sighed in relief. "I'm sorry," she said as she stepped back toward the window. But a piece of slate gave way under her—she crashed hard against the roof and slid until the heel of her boot caught the gutter, which groaned and bent under her weight.

Franklin lurched forward and grabbed at the soldier's wrist just as the gutter gave way. Her legs slid over the edge and she dangled there in Franklin's grasp. He relaxed his fingers for just a split second in an effort to get a better grip on her forearm, but her damp skin slipped out of his grasp—she fell from the second-story ledge. Franklin heard a thud and a snap that he hoped was just a board, or maybe the trunk of a shrub breaking under her weight. But when he heard that god-awful scream, he knew it was her body that had broken. He looked over the edge and saw her clutching at a thighbone that bent as though her right leg had a second knee.

Franklin ducked back through the window, ran downstairs and outside. He opened the passenger door of his truck, returned to scoop her up, and without stopping to collect his suitcase or gun, he placed her in the seat, left the Jeep behind, and flew down the access road toward the county lane. He left his home without so much as a rearview glance.

•

The town was deserted—not even so much as a police cruiser in sight. Ezekiel breathed deep, tried to keep calm as he raced down Ohio Street, then turned onto Broad. Past boarded-up buildings, the empty pharmacy—which had been loaded into moving vans days ago, the drugs shipped off to safety before even the first people were. His knees ached, and his arms felt strained and weary under the weight of their suitcases.

It was ten past five when they reached the gate, but a bottleneck of waiting cars kept the tunnel open. Soldiers shouted at drivers and horns blared—Ezekiel ignored it all until he was inside the tunnel and past the gate. Only then did he slow to a walk; Jade went skipping ahead while he caught his breath. "Stay with me," he said, and Jade turned around and came back to him with her bottom lip jutting out in a pout. Ezekiel looked up at the 40-foot wall of concrete, the four-foot-thick steel gate that would seal the town, separate the peninsula from the main landmass of Illinois. Outside the gates, pickup trucks and cars maneuvered around—drivers shouted and chose routes, paused before hitting the open road to reinforce the lines of twine and rope and chain that fastened their belongings to vehicle roofs. People shouted out the names of hotels rumored to have vacancies seventy or a hundred miles up the road. Churches that might provide shelter, or relatives with extra beds. Roadways that had been washed out or were impassable or had recently reopened. Junk littered the road—possessions that had fallen off vehicles, or had been discarded in favor of some more important item, or maybe an extra passenger. Ezekiel looked away from it all. He dropped the luggage on the ground and took a seat on one bag; Jade sat on the other, and they waited. They waited until all the cars had left, their neighbors, their friends— good kind people who would normally have stopped just to chat. But now, in the flurry of leaving, no one stopped for Jade and

Ezekiel, or any of the handful of others who sat outside the gate—the carless, the lost.

Ezekiel held tight to Jade when the gears wailed and the gate screeched down its track. He watched it descend, covering up his city—his home—until it pressed tightly into place. Cairo was sealed off, left as an offering to the river. Somewhere in a courtroom, someone was deciding between Birds Point and Cairo, between land and city, between poor and poorer, and he had a good idea how the axe would fall. He sat quietly with his daughter and tried to believe Ed's words, tried to believe things were *good*.

•

It was dark when James Smith arrived at the wall. A blond soldier with a sour expression on his face waved him to a stop. The boy—he didn't look a week past eighteen—pointed a flashlight through James' windshield, straight into his eyes.

James squinted and cranked his window down by hand. The soldier walked up, poked the flashlight around the car and said "Road's closed." He chomped a wad of chewing gum and his breath smelled like rotten strawberries.

"I gathered that," James said. "Just here to pick up my family."

The soldier left the window, aimed his flashlight into the truck bed. James squeezed the steering wheel tight. Tired from the trip, nervous to find Ezekiel and Jade, he bit his lip. He didn't need any trouble.

"You can park on the shoulder there and take a quick look around. Not many folks left."

"Thank you, sir," James said. He tried not to let it sound as sarcastic as it felt.

He jumped out of the truck and walked past some sort of makeshift command post—a white open-sided tent full of cops and soldiers with walkie-talkies strapped to their belts. He walked past a satellite truck and a couple of reporters who lingered, tapping out stories on laptops and talking on cell phones. In a Red Cross tent, volunteers dished out meals to the other relief workers, but the actual residents—the people everyone was supposed to be helping—were scattered beneath the city limits sign and next to the clamped gate. Some milled around, some slept on the pavement. James saw faces that looked vaguely familiar, but after 15 years he couldn't think of names, and he didn't care to.

Ezekiel was in the back of the stragglers, leaning on the post of a street sign with Jade asleep in his arms, looking serene as can be. "Thought I'd never get here," James said.

Ezekiel nodded but didn't move. He looked beat, and then some. "That thought had occurred to me, as well." He stood slowly, careful not to wake Jade as he lifted her. James picked up the suitcases.

•

Lieutenant Brown hardly made a noise as Franklin drove her. He repeated, "I'm sorry, I'm sorry," until it became clear she did not intend to respond. He glanced right to check on her every few seconds, and could see the strain in her cheek and neck muscles, the way she clenched her fists even more tightly every time the truck struck a bump in the lopsided tar-and-chip road. She did not speak until they passed the setback levee, the one designed to keep the river's overflow trapped on Franklin's land and away from more heavily populated areas. This was the wall that would turn his home into a lakebed. "Slow down," she said, and then rolled down her window.

"What the hell?" asked the soldier who stood guard at the gate. "Where's your—"

"We're the last ones," she said. "Seal it." She struggled to pull a sheet of paper from her back pocket. She showed him the order and he nodded, then rushed off.

She turned to Franklin and said, "Drive." The flimsy country road ended in a T-joint at the state route. Four miles north, across a bridge made impassable by the high water, was the nearest hospital—Cairo General. He shook his head at this realization and steered left, south, for the 20-mile trip to

Sikeston. As he accelerated, she pulled a radio receiver from her belt.

"We're out," she said. "Gate's down. Blow it."

Franklin clamped his teeth and kicked the gas pedal even harder.

When they arrived, Franklin pulled into the Emergency bay, fetched a wheelchair, and pushed through the automatic doors of Missouri Delta Medical Center. He handed her a clipboard to check in, and told her he'd park and be back in a moment.

"Just go," she said. "Now. If you so much step back into this hospital, I'll call the police." Franklin opened his mouth to argue, but her cold stare told him not to bother. He climbed into his truck and drove off. Janie and the girls were safe with relatives in Springfield and he knew he should call them, let them know he'd made it out all right. They would be worried, he knew. They would be watching the news, maybe even live video. But instead of looking for a payphone, he drove back to the setback levee and parked his truck at a spot where the chip-and-tar road dead-ended at a steel gate. He climbed a footpath up the levee and waited. This is where it would all become lake, where it would all become wasted, everything he and his neighbors had worked their whole lives to cultivate.

He sat on that earthen wall for just a few moments before a series of bright, golden charges lit up the pitch-black sky. A rolling volley of loud booms followed closely behind, and a few seconds later, a scent close to that of gunpowder reached him. Someone not waiting for devastation would have seen it like low-slung fireworks: sharp, powerful, almost beautiful. He cringed at this thought and dismissed it. Franklin pushed the *illuminate* button on his digital wristwatch, and switched it to stopwatch mode and then waited. He wanted to know just how quickly a man's life could be washed away.

•

As Captain Abrams motored north past Cairo, he saw his men rushing toward the starboard railing, leaning forward, pointing. He took his eyes off the river ahead of him, aimed his spotlight away from the channel and toward the bank. He knew better than this. He knew his focus should be on the waterway. But still he turned, and from his perch two stories above river level, he saw a small wedge of sandbags cave inward, toward the city. Then, as if yanked away by some great, unseen hand, the whole network of bags toppled, earthen walls crumbled, pieces of concrete splashed into water as it rushed past the defeated levee. He veered toward the left channel, far from the breach, from what levee remained, and kicked the propellers to full speed, putting as much distance as possible between his ship and the wash. He turned his spotlight toward the opposite bank to watch for obstructions, to seek out the clearest channel—and that's when he saw out of the corner of his eye the flashes of dynamite charge, the low set of golden sparks. He inhaled and turned backward; his hands slipped from the wheel, and then he grabbed it again, more concerned with steadying himself than the boat. They'd waited too long—water had spilled over *both* sides. City and crops—all of it gone. With trembling fingers, he reached again for the wrinkled copy of his orders, searching for answers, for understanding, for explanation, for an idea of what would come next. He looked to his left and right—no escort this time, no help. He pointed a spotlight on the black water ahead, gripped the wheel and drove his boat forward, away.

the shore of erie

I would have preferred to wait and fly in for the funeral, but Sarah convinced me to see him while he was still breathing. She made a compelling argument: "I'm not paying the therapy if you don't see him."

I shrugged, as I do when she's so correct that I've got no rebuttal, and then shuffled off to pack some casual clothes and a funeral suit. I knew the suit he'd choose as his last clothing: a tired navy-blue Sears number with a lapel as wide as Montana. Any time he ever had to get dressed up, that's the one he picked. He accumulated suits over the years—I even sent a couple that fit him properly, but all those others just collected mothballs in favor of the polyester monstrosity. I opened my closet, where the suits hung in order, dark to light. From what Mom had said on the phone, the man was tired and ready to go, so black didn't seem wholly appropriate. I didn't want to steal any thunder from his blue—or maybe didn't want to be associated with it—so I reached dead center and pulled out a simple gray suit, then the two shades that flanked it, for good measure.

Sarah said she'd fly into Pittsburgh when it came time for the funeral. The kids, she said, hadn't known their grandfather well enough to spend God-knows-how-long moping at the man's bedside. That was, apparently, my responsibility

"Make sure you get some skating in," I told Andrew. "Tryouts in two weeks."

"I'm well aware," he said, then turned to glare at the ridiculous red circle I'd drawn around tryout day on the kitchen calendar. It had seemed a good idea at the time.

"Just make sure you're ready," I said. "This is your year for varsity."

"Yes, sir," he said, and sulked off. I hugged Sarah and left.

I weaved through our suburb, Tanglewood—which was laid out, apparently to mimic its name—and steered the car east, pointed it downhill toward sea level, off our safe Denver mountaintop, down toward the south shore of Lake Erie.

On the way to Denver 10 years earlier, I stuck to four-laners the whole way, the cruise control set to 15-over as I put a dozen states and every possible foot of altitude between us. For this return trip, though, I swiped Sarah's treasured McNally atlas from her beige minivan and used a black marker to plot a route that snaked down the thinnest roads fit for mapping. I knew I'd have to buy her a new atlas, that she'd find my markings and folded page corners just as unacceptable as the idea of listening to the voice from her phone telling her where to go.

I piloted my black Mercedes (the car he dismissed as flashy and excessive) through the plains. I drove down the center of one-and-a-half lane roads, no opposing traffic for miles on end. I watched out the side windows as machines chewed bronze fields and spat them into silos. Winding through parts of America that had no business being involved with this trip, I became the sort of driver I most despise, loping below the posted speed and invoking great numbers of honks from fellow travelers as I refused to pass creeping farm implements. I watched the gangly arms of Nebraska center-pivots stretch across vast fields toward what felt like the edges of Earth, and I was happy to copy their nearly imperceptible slowness.

When bells rang at railroad crossings, I eased off the gas instead of rushing forward to beat the gates. The trains with four engines were best—they pulled strings of cars that stretched to one end of the horizon when the gate went down and then reached the other by the time the gate rose. It's amazing how much hydrochloric acid cuts north through the plains and how much corn syrup rolls south.

Farther east, I wondered why it is that some trees grow so bright in autumn, and others fade so dull. I stopped at ridiculous tourist traps—a 50-foot-tall teepee in Kansas, Carhenge in Nebraska, even a house shaped like an ice cream cone in Illinois. These were the types of places that had set my eyes rolling when

Sarah piloted family trips, places where I pretended to sleep while she and the kids explored.

I stood beneath the Gateway arch at twilight and marveled at how terrifyingly ugly and corroded it looks in the wrong light. St. Louis seemed like a place that often wore the wrong light. I slept at one-story motels with pink neon vacancy signs and ate greasy T-bones at truck stops, all the while knowing that when I finally got on with it, I'd find Mom sitting in that same spot on the porch, that she'd lead me to a twin bed covered in the same white sheets (not with Sarah's hospital corners, but with Mom's plain, regular tuck under the mattress), that she'd probably even have a roast and tea waiting on the table.

On the fourth morning, I dragged my feet one last time and walked through the bombed-out downtown of Youngstown, Ohio. People there live in the shadows of the steel mills where they once worked, hulking rust dinosaurs that litter the skyline and color every moment of existence. I wondered why they didn't just demolish the things and start over, but then I considered my own trip and figured we were sharing the great rustbelt futility: the fruitless wait for last-minute changes despite the inevitable. That's when I gave up, broke down, got on with it.

•

Mom was knitting on the porch when I arrived. I pretended not to see her, pretended to miss the driveway and turned around at the cul-de-sac—made a second pass. I pulled in and there she was, wearing her too-warm smile, one that said everything I knew she'd avoid in conversation.

"It has been a while, I suppose."

"Hi, Mom."

I reached in to hug her, and she wrapped one arm around me, gave my back a quick pat and stood.

"Hungry?" she asked, then opened the door and walked in. I followed. "Of course you are. Made a roast the other day. Figured you'd take your time getting here, so I made something that kept well. Cheesecake's in the deep freeze. That's in the basement, you'll remember, which can be accessed through that door right there." She pointed, and I trudged off to fetch dessert. By the time I got back, she'd already taken my bag to my old bedroom.

She always liked meals to seem pleasant, so she told me about the neighbors while we ate, paltry things neither of us cared about, like how the Thompsons had filled in their old swimming pool and how the Andersons had put their place on the market with plans to move south, to Florida, maybe. While she talked, my eyes kept wandering to the closed door at the end of the hall.

After the cheesecake, I grabbed the plates and took them to the sink.

"So that wife of yours finally taught you how to wash a dish," Mom said. "I must've underestimated her."

"I think you did. Her name is still Sarah, by the way."

"She wouldn't have been my first choice. The Davis girl is still single, you know. Pretty little blond, that one. Full of spirit."

"Full of a few things I don't think you'd want me to catch." I should have left it at that, but I added, "She's more Evan's type." I stopped myself before mentioning how often she *had* been Evan's type.

Mom shook her head and walked off toward the old man's bedroom. When she returned, I was drying the last beige plate, tracing with a towel the green pinstripe on its rim, remembering the way those pinstripes framed our meals before Sarah and her gleaming white tableware arrived in my life.

"He's asleep," she said, then nodded toward the back door. "Go wander around a bit, get your bearings back. I'll come get you if he wakes at a decent hour."

From the back porch, I watched the sun retreat across Lake Erie. The opposite shore wasn't quite visible, but the light halo cast by Buffalo hovered over the water. With nothing but sky and water before me, this had always been the one place where I swore I could actually see the earth curve. A familiar breeze swept my hair upward, revealed significantly more forehead than the last time I stood there. I walked to the shore through grass I'd never seen so unruly—four inches tall and uneven with a handful of blighted spots where the sandy earth stood cracked and bald.

Then, I saw the boat slip. Its planks stood rotted and decayed, nearly consumed by weeds and reeds. But it held shape and form, defiant against those lapping waves. An entire winter, my first season of varsity, he'd skipped every last hockey game to sit home, drawing up plans and pre-cutting boards in the garage. He went all-out on that damn thing—bought drafting paper, mechanical pencils, a new compass, an enormous T-square. It was a midlife crisis without gearshifts. I don't know what got him set upon it, but once he started, it was unbridled obsession. That spring, convinced he'd grow tired of his project and be overcome by desire to catch up on lost sport-related bonding time, I signed up for baseball. I hated baseball, and he didn't come to a game. Mom showed up to a few—she sat alone in the bleachers and looked up from her romance novels when it was time for me to strike out. Meanwhile, Evan stayed home and helped him build while I kicked at every right field anthill in the northwest district.

He came inside to meet my prom date in a tank top and his work belt. He extended toward her a hand caked in sweat and sawdust, which set that night on a predictably irredeemable path. All spring he worked on that thing—*they* worked on it. While I was flailing miserably at the last three pitches of our lone tournament game, Dad and Evan were overseeing the delivery of a weathered old 12-foot sailboat, bought from a classified ad.

Mrs. Thompkins dropped me off just in time for me to catch Evan smashing a bottle of Iron City beer over its hull. They had the thing fifty yards out into the lake before either one of them noticed me standing there. Dad waved and shouted something to me, something I couldn't make out—though there may have been a lack of effort on my part. I didn't stand there long enough to find out whether or not they came back to shore for me. That night I waited until I could distinctly hear all three of them snoring and then made for the kitchen. I stole an Iron City can from the crisper drawer, drank it, and snuck out the back door to christen the vessel my own way. I never did go to sleep that night. Instead, I lay there converting everything that'd ever happened in our house to some evil plot against me.

That was the night I understood I'd been excluded from my father's existence. And in response, I excluded myself from his. My family has always had problems with patterns. Just like the rest of them, we ignored this one, never bothered to try fixing it until the last minute.

•

"How is he?"

Mom closed the door to his room, and I heard her footsteps tracing the house behind me until she reached the kitchen.

"He's awake, about as lucid as he's going to be. Tea?"

I was drinking coffee as a stand-in for breakfast. She was sleeping when I woke, and so I'd already made a trip to the Starbucks on Lake Street. I downed the last bit and shoved the cup down inside a trashcan, pushed a piece of newspaper over it so she wouldn't see and get indignant.

"Of course."

"Lipton's okay? Or do I need to go to the market for some of that froofy—"

"Lipton's is fine."

I listened to her calm cadence. Despite the wall between us, I knew she was opening the right cupboard door and then the left one. Pans moved with a gentle clatter as she slid them aside to reach for the kettle—always hidden in the back despite being the most-used item in the kitchen.

"Lake's lovely this morning, Mom. Just the slightest hint of a whitecap out by—"

"I figured that's where you'd gone." She walked to the doorway and leaned against the frame as she pulled teabags out of paper wrappers. I didn't tell her that I was actually looking

147

forward to drinking plain black tea that wasn't organic, fruit-infused or meant to awaken some sort of inner awareness.

"Lake's always where you ran off when you wanted to hide," she said. "Decades don't change much, do they—aside from putting more lines on your face?"

"You didn't expect me to come home and stay put in one spot, did you?"

"It's just the timing, that's all. The morning he's got his wits about him, you're barefoot strolling."

I was past arguing, though I had a feeling that it had become her primary vessel for showing affection. I suspected she'd forgotten how to do it any other way.

"He still awake?"

She nodded. *Then, no harm done*, I wanted to tell her, but it would've accomplished nothing. I checked a clock—I hadn't been gone an hour.

I stood and walked to his room, turned the handle without pausing and walked in. He seemed to be asleep, but I touched his shoulder, just in case. It was warm, and when squeezed more tightly, I felt the slightest trace of a pulse

"Dad?" I whispered, and he didn't answer. Mom had the curtains pulled so tight that the room was nearly dark. I couldn't see anything outside the triangle of light that projected through the doorway. I sat on the bed next to him, tried to think up what I might say to him when he woke, if he woke—I realized I hadn't spent a single mile of that trip planning for this or preparing myself for what it would be like. I watched his chest rise and fall meekly until Mom tapped at the door and whispered, "Tea's ready." I patted his mattress before I stood, then told him, "Best talk we've had in years."

•

I went back in after tea and Mom's sugar cookies (which were better than I remembered—somehow, less plain). Mom had the curtains drawn so the sun came straight in. It was so bright I could see particles of dust suspended in the air. I stood in the doorway until my eyes adjusted, then looked around his room. It

was jarring to see his silver pocket watch resting on his dresser—
it was the first time I'd seen it separated from his person; that
chain had always been visible and connected. Even as he built
the slip, that watch chain always hung from the pocket of his
work jeans.

The rest of the room seemed largely unchanged: sparse and
pristine with a soft musky smell. On his bookshelf rested a row
of volumes I knew he'd never read, arranged in order of size.
Some of Mom's things were still in the room, though she'd been
sleeping across the hall for months. I stepped further into the
room and the tired oak floor groaned under my foot. From the
center of his sleigh bed, he opened his eyes and turned toward
me.

"Dad?"

He struggled to sit up. I wedged a pillow under his back to
hold him there. His eyes were sunken, and the lines in his face
deeper, but I half expected him to leap out of bed and order me
to gas up the mower. Instead, he just stared blankly.

"Dad?" I asked again. I sat down on the corner of his bed
closest to the door.

"Evan, that you?" he asked. "Good of you to come, son.
Good of you to come. Your mother needs help with the chores,
me being all laid up like this."

"Dad, it's Jake. I just drove in from Colorado—"

"Just because my eyes aren't working good doesn't mean you
can pull one on me."

He chuckled, but that turned into an extended cough. He
grabbed a glass of water off his bedside table and took a drink,
half of which spilled down his shirt.

"Let me get that for you," I said, looking around the room
for some sort of rag or towel.

"I can take care of myself. Now, Evan, tell me how—"

"It's *Jake*. It's me. Mom asked me to come...home."

"Stop covering for your brother," he said, his voice growing harsh. "The boy quit us. Up and left us behind. You quit talking about him."

I didn't believe him, and this irritated me. If he was messing with me, that was irritating in itself. But more difficult was the realization that in this, of all moments, I didn't know whether I could trust him.

"Fine, Dad. Fine. Can I get you anything?"

"A cigar and some whiskey might be nice."

"I don't know if that'd be appropriate right now," I said.

"Christ, you *do* sound like Jake."

I got him distracted talking about the Steelers, then sat and listened to that train of thought disintegrate into a rant about Democrats, which flowed right into a rant about goose droppings that were ruining his lawn. I nodded and tried to make sense of it, sat there and waited until I smelled the lunch Mom was making in the kitchen.

"I'm going to go help her, Pop. I'll be back." He said nothing, and I walked out.

I set the kitchen table, while she stirred a pan of pasta sauce.

"Is he screwing with me, or can he really not remember?"

"Does it really matter?"

•

I went back in the afternoon, with a new thought in the back of my head: maybe he was smarter than I'd given him credit for. Maybe he was using Evan to say the things he couldn't say otherwise. To apologize, to put things right. And so I walked in, hopeful, ready to listen. I took him coffee—Mom wouldn't have approved, but I figured it couldn't hurt.

He took the mug and smiled a sly smile, nodded at me. He set it on the bedside table.

"Thank you," he said. "She never lets me have anything fun anymore."

"Don't tell her I brought it."

He slid his thumb and forefinger across his lips as if zipping them, then flicked his imaginary key toward the coffee.

"There anything in it?"

"Just sugar."

"Damn."

I kept waiting for him to address me, or Evan—someone. I got nothing.

"How are your pillows?"

He shrugged, didn't say anything.

"Need anything else?"

He shook his head slightly.

I tried not to get mad, tried to be patient, tried to wait out the silence. I would've preferred he sit up and call me a useless bastard. But I just sat there staring at him, and he stared at the ceiling. The coffee stopped steaming, went cool. He fell asleep, and still I waited. When Mom called for me, I lingered for another moment. I knew I should tell him I loved him. I started to, but nothing came out. My lips refused to move. It hurt a little just to think this, to admit it to myself. I couldn't tell it to even a sleeping man who couldn't hear and couldn't care.

I stood and leaned to kiss him on the forehead, then tiptoed my way out so the man could rest. I paused to run my right index finger over his watch, and shuddered at how cold it felt, so far from its place. I pulled the door shut behind me and leaned against it, shut my eyes, and tried to replay the whole tiny, dumb conversation about coffee, to brand it so firmly into my mind that it would never escape. I hugged Mom, then took another walk. When I reached the beach, I took off my shoes and walked for miles barefoot, chinos rolled halfway up my calves. I wrote an internal speech, tabulated all the things I wanted to tell him, the apologies I felt compelled to give and the forgiveness that he'd shrug off anyway. He hated sentiments of that sort—they both did. I drafted the monologue again and again, knowing how pointless it was, knowing that if he had anything nearing his wits about him, he'd tell me after two minutes to stop blubbering, then he'd change the conversation to something about tools and engines and the names of race car drivers, the sorts of things I was supposed to understand but never got around to caring about. I revised it over and over until I stubbed my toe on a buried rock and realized I'd be better served by paying attention to the familiar but quite distant place around me. Soon, I'd have a wife and kids to tour around my hometown. The kids probably wouldn't even remember their last visit and Sarah wouldn't remember much more than the way she put on pearls for a "fancy" (Mom's word) family dinner that turned out to be at Golden Corral. Dad wore his blue suit to that one, and during the awkward gaps in conversation that punctuated our night, I tabulated an even number of snide remarks and giggles directed toward the born and chosen parts of my family. If last time was any indication, I needed to relish these last minutes alone.

I walked up the peninsula, where bad pop music blared from the beach concession stands. Kids just off school for the day were trying to squeeze a few final minutes out of the summer with Frisbees and footballs and beach towels. I called home, told Sarah that Dad was still hanging on, that Mom hadn't changed a bit. She reassured me Andrew was keeping up with both practice and school. She said the school's baseball coach had cornered him in the hall and told him he had the build of a power hitter, and that the team was lacking just such a player—that he could be a star.

"What'd he say?" I asked. I'd stopped walking, slightly nervous.

"He told me he shook coach's hand, thanked him, then said, 'baseball's boring.'"

"Good boy," I said, and started walking again. "Is he around?"

"Nah," she said. "He's at the rink."

I looked at my watch and calculated the time distance. I knew she was lying, and smiled, shook my head. We talked for a couple more minutes, then she told me she had some errands to run and hung up.

When I ran out of beach to walk, I put my shoes back on, and went downtown. All my old hangouts had become something else, or had been boarded up. I walked into one place that called itself a coffee shop but just saw some Styrofoam cups on a counter and a couple old ladies watching game shows on a tube television. Even the Taste Freeze had been plowed under. That place had been ancient when I was a kid, so it didn't surprise me that the ramshackle building was gone. But it irked me to see a sterile, boxy Dairy Queen standing in its place. I peeked through the window, saw all those swarthy, logoed cups sitting behind the counter instead of the strewn boxes of waffle cones that had once seemed so alluring. I was glad to see the place empty. Served them right.

Second Presbyterian church had been turned into the kind of bar that sells Coronas by the bucket, and the bar that used to sell Coronas by the bucket now appeared to sell its employees' affection by the song.

The Ben Franklin, which had held on so much longer than its contemporaries, now rested vacant with a Realtor's face plastered all over the windows. Across the street, the beige corrugated majesty of the county's newest Dollar General. Mops were on sale. And pool noodles.

"Evan worked a double shift at the plant yesterday," Mom told me when I got home. "So he'll stop by for dinner tonight."

That was Mom's code for, "Evan stops by every night and I cook for him."

I smiled, or tried to. With no mirrors nearby, I couldn't be certain of how it came out. "Sounds nice," I said.

•

Evan wore a camouflage shirt and a bright orange hat. He stunk, but I couldn't figure out what the smell was.

"It's not deer season, is it?"

He leaned back in his chair and laughed. Mom smiled at him.

"It's *always* deer season, long as no one catches you."

I rolled my eyes.

"Where do you think dinner came from?" Mom asked.

"Christ, this is deer?" I scooted back from the table.

Evan gave Mom a soft punch on the shoulder. "He's just as gullible as ever, isn't he? Why would I waste perfectly good venison on you?"

"He has a good point," Mom said.

"Cute, guys," I said. "Just don't pull this on Sarah."

"We'll leave the lady be," Evan said. Besides, she doesn't need our help figuring out she's too good for you. She'll put that together on her own, someday."

I stopped the conversation by eating, which reminded him there was food, and he turned his attention to the plate. That's always been the best way to shut him up—remind him that there's food. There weren't five words between us the rest of the meal.

We both helped with the dishes—Mom washing, Evan rinsing, me drying, and for a moment, it felt familiar and not entirely terrible.

After we finished, Mom went for a walk around the block. "Doctor's orders," she lied, then left us there to try and put up with each other.

"He thinks I'm you," I told him, after he'd flipped through half the satellite channels. He settled on a wildlife show and turned toward me, scrunched his brow.

"Seriously?"

"I don't know. Keeps calling me Evan."

"Of all the things for him to scramble, I would've bet he'd keep us straight. What's he telling you? Or me. Or whoever."

"He keeps telling Evan to hide his watch so Jake doesn't take it," I said.

Evan rolled his eyes. "Him and that stupid watch. I don't get the fixation. Yeah—it's supposed to be mine."

"Are you kidding?" I leaned forward away from the plush sofa back.

He shrugged. "The hell am I going to do with it? I've got a phone if I need to keep time. It's useless."

"But he loved that watch. I mean—"

"Listen, mister sentimental. You want it? Make me an offer. Otherwise, I pawn the thing and buy some beer."

"You'd trade Dad's favorite possession for beer."

"You don't even like him. What do you care?"

I felt my fists clench and looked away. I couldn't remember feeling angrier than in that moment—the beloved son shrugging off his father's favor. Or maybe it was just that our angst had grown so engrained we were willing to take opposite sides on any issue, even a dying father. I took a deep breath, then asked, "How much beer?"

He laughed and punched me in the shoulder, hard enough to sting but not bruise.

"I'd say that'll take a couple cases."

"How many?"

"What kind of beer? Hell—you're serious, aren't you?"

"How many?"

He leaned back in his seat, then looked at me and raised his eyebrows. "Okay," he said. "Two cases of Iron City, and the watch is yours."

Without a word, I stood up and walked out the front door, got in my car, backed out without looking and nearly hit a Ford that was zipping down the street. The driver honked and flipped me off. Evan stood in the doorway, shaking his head and smirking. I bought the beer without listening to the total price—just handed over a fifty and took whatever change he handed me. I drove back and placed it into the cluttered bed of his rusted Chevy pickup.

He reached out his hand when I walked back into the living room, and as much as it repulsed me, I reached out mine, and we shook.

We went in together—all three of us—before Evan went home for the evening. Mom stood in the middle, an arm around each of us. I could've sworn Dad was awake, but his eyes stayed shut. I imagine he wanted the awkward family moment to end as much as we did, but for Mom, we stood, together, one last time, all four of us breathing softly at our own pace. Evan left first, and on his way out, he flicked the watch with his index finger, sent it sliding across the dresser. It just barely clung to the edge, narrowly missing a plunge to the floor that probably would've destroyed it.

Mom said nothing to him, but pushed it back from the edge on her way out. I leaned over and kissed Dad on the forehead then paused on the way out, watched the watch's tired old hands labor to keep spinning.

•

When I finished my shower the next morning, she was sitting at the table, waiting for me, with a mug of tea for each of us, and toast. We ate fairly quietly. She asked about my day, I asked about hers. I told her I'd just talked to Sarah, who had said hello. None of this was true, of course, but I knew that in a few days I'd need them to put up with each other, or at least create that appearance. She washed the dishes and I dried them—by then it felt routine again—and then I walked down the hallway toward his room. I heard her footsteps behind me, and before I could reach for the doorknob, she said, "Don't." I turned around to ask why, but she didn't wait.

"He's not doing well today. Let him rest. You can see him tonight, maybe."

"Can I at least sit by—"

"Just leave him be," she said, then turned away, walked into the living room.

I heard the television come on, and under the cover of its noise I turned the doorknob anyway and took a step inside. I stopped by the dresser and watched him for a moment, so frail and distant in the middle of that huge bed. She had blinds and curtains pulled down tight again to dim the room—she seemed to have some sort of schedule for this, but I hadn't figured it out. I caught one glint of brightness—the hallway light bouncing off the edge of the pocket watch. I finally picked it up and for the first time in my life felt its remarkable weight—so much more substantial than the steel and titanium face wrapped around my own wrist. I thought about placing it in my own pocket—not for good, just to see how it would feel, how that weight would affect me. Instead, I wrapped my fingers tight around it, prayed the floorboards wouldn't give me away, and tiptoed to his side. On the bedside table sat the coffee I'd brought him the day before, still untouched. His nose whistled slightly every time he exhaled, and his lips were chapped and broken. His shave was uneven, his pajamas were loose against his pale frame. He looked awful, and I made myself stand there and see him. After a moment, I reached down, placed the watch in his hand where it belonged and closed his fingers around it.

I wanted to run through the whole speech I'd composed on the beach but decided that could wait. Maybe he'd hear me then. Maybe, he'd understand. I decided to give him the condensed version.

"You could be a bastard sometimes," I said. "But I really can't help loving you."

I walked out, not caring what the floorboards did. I'm sure they squeaked, and I'm sure Mom heard them, but she didn't rustle or make a peep as I walked through the kitchen and out the back door.

In the ramshackle shed, hidden behind tufts of cobweb, the hand mower was fueled up—God knows how long that gasoline had been in there, but it started up just fine and I made each pass neat and straight as I could, marching back and forth across the dewy lawn. At one point, I saw Mom in the window, and I couldn't make out from her expression whether she was scolding me for the noise or thanking me for the work. It might have been both in the same look, for all I'd ever been able to sort. In the trees that surrounded me as I worked, I no longer saw contrast—the bright and the somber—but instead, saw them unified and barren. I paused in the middle of the lawn and looked up at his window. I wondered if he, too, was watching me, thought I knew how unlikely it was he could have moved himself to the window.

Still, a part of me hoped. I wanted to know he was paying attention. I wanted, just once, to see him smile—to hear him thank me. I wanted to hear the man speak, just when I knew it was least likely. Instead, I pushed forward, cut path after path from his failing lawn.

I surveyed the work from the back porch, and knew the lines weren't crisp enough. Dad wouldn't have approved, anyway. I thought about the zigzags I'd drawn all over my wife's map, my crooked swings at a childhood full of fastballs—how straight lines and I had so frequently avoided each other. And I imagined that somewhere, sealed up in an envelope inside some lawyer's files, was a document stating that my father had willed me his T-square. I raked and bagged the clippings, thought about how Sarah would have made me throw them into compost. I pulled my cell phone from my pocket and turned it on, but stopped short of dialing to tell her I missed her. She was still asleep, I knew. I grabbed a pair of lawn shears from the garage. They took a moment to find—Dad hung his tools in alphabetical order, so I checked the "L" section before finding them in section "S", right next to the (tomato) stakes. As the sun pulled itself upward from the horizon, I set about clearing reeds and cattails from the warped, moldy remains of the boat slip. I groomed that shore to the syncopated waves. The shears creaked with each squeeze of the handles; the vegetation whispered with each slice. Grasshoppers chirped, lightning bugs blinked and frogs let out their throaty moans. Any other morning, the dissonance would've been maddening—I would've raced for the first set of earphones I could find. But in that moment, the noise was right.

Having cleared the slip of overgrowth, I decided to scale those boards once more, maybe even dangle my toes for a moment in the cool, dark water.

There was no slumping, no sound or warning of any sort—on my third step, the tired wood beams underneath me snapped, shrugged, and plunged into the shallow edge of Lake Erie. I landed hard on my back and hit my head on a board. I lay in the lake, surrounded by the wreckage, then used the last upright piling to hoist myself up.

I pulled one of the broken timbers from the water and remembered the hands that had so carefully crafted the slip, hands that had weathered alongside the wood. I knew that when I turned around, I would see my mother standing on the back porch with her arms folded and a vacant expression on her face, that it would be time to call Sarah and arrange a flight. That the watch now belonged to me. And so I remained frozen, the water lapping at my shins, broken boards jutting through the surface at all angles. I squeezed the plank in my hand, a piece of two-by-ten the length of my forearm, sawed at one end and splintered at the other. I pulled a penny nail from the broken end and held it—still smooth and gray after all these years and so many waves. I dropped the board back into the water. Coat after coat, decades of waterproofing remained diligent and kept it afloat. I watched the timber bob back and forth among the ruins, uncertain whether to beach itself right here, or to float off in search of something else.

acknowledgements

This book would not have been completed without the gracious gifts of time and space to create, afforded chiefly by the graduate program in creative writing at Southern Illinois University Carbondale; the Breadloaf Bakeless Nason Endowment and the Camargo Foundation in Cassis, France; the U.S. Department of State's Fulbright Program; and Novosibirsk State Pedagogical University.

I thank my publisher and editor Garrett Dennert for his encouragement, patience and thoughtful treatment of these stories. I thank the journal and magazine editors who have cared for previous versions of these stories and given them attention, space, and audience. I thank my gracious and most trusted readers—including but not limited to Lane Kareska, Angela Palm, Derand Wright, and Katie Darby-Mullins—without whom these stories could not have found their best shapes.

Most of all, I am grateful to my parents, brother, and dear wife Rachael, for the things no word or page can produce: for love and care, unconditional goodness, expectation and understanding.

Brooks Rexroat was raised near Cincinnati, Ohio at the intersection of the Rust Belt and Appalachia: the crossing point of mountain and farm field, boarded mine and shuttered factory, the water that splits north from south. The importance of place has always surrounded him, and it deeply inhabits his characters.

After earning a Master of Fine Arts Degree in creative prose from Southern Illinois University Carbondale, he embarked on a journey in higher education that has included teaching opportunities at open enrollment community colleges, regional public universities, and rigorous private liberal arts colleges. Now based at Brescia University in Western Kentucky, Rexroat spent the 2016-2017 academic year as a Fulbright U.S. Teaching and Research Scholar at Novosibirsk State Pedagogical University in Siberia, Russia. He was a 2014 Bread Loaf Bakeless Camargo Fellow in Cassis, France and his stories and essays have appeared in more than 30 journals and magazines on three continents.

story acknowledgements

"Blood Off Rusted Steel"
First published in *Best of Ohio Short Stories Volume One*.

"Angel of Death"
First published in *The Telegraph* Short Story Competition.

"Moving Day"
First published in *Weave Magazine*.

"Destroying New Boston"
First published in *The Cleveland Review*. Anthologized in *Every River on Earth: Writing From Appalachian Ohio*

"Conventions"
First published in *Midwestern Gothic*, issue eight.

"Miss Ellen Told Me"
First published in *Best of Ohio Short Stories Volume II*.

"Basement Party"
First published in *The Montreal Review*.

"Five Meals in Paris"
First published in *Jet Fuel Review*.

"Waiting Out the Apocalypse"
First published in *Big Muddy: A Journal of the Mississippi River Valley*

"The Shore of Erie"
First published in *Marathon Literary Review*.

Orson's Publishing is an independent book publisher operating out of Seattle, Washington. Founded in 2016, Orson's delivers wise, yet approachable storytelling to readers everywhere. For more information, please visit orsonspublishing.com.

CPSIA information can be obtained
at www.ICGtesting.com
Printed in the USA
LVHW04s1620300518
578989LV00004B/774/P